A Glossary of Magic and Wonder, Vol. 1

Christopher Sans

The role of the book within our culture is changing. The change is brought on by new ways to acquire & use content, the rapid dissemination of information and real-time peer collaboration on a global scale. Despite these changes one thing is clear--"the book" in it's traditional form continues to play an important role in learning and communication. The book you are holding in your hands utilizes the unique characteristics of the Internet -- relying on web infrastructure and collaborative tools to share and use resources in keeping with the characteristics of the medium (user-created, defying control, etc.)--while maintaining all the convenience and utility of a real book.

Contents

Articles

A   **1**

Abbey of Thelema	1
Abramelin oil	4
Adept	11
Akashic records	14
Alchemy	16
Ascended master	25
Astral projection	29
Astrology	36
Automatic writing	53

B   **55**

Banishing	55
Bibliomancy	56
Biosophy	59
Black magic	61
Subtle body	64

C   **73**

Candomblé	73
Cartomancy	82
Clairvoyance	84
Collective unconscious	92
Coven	94
Charmstone	96

| Chakra | 97 |

References

| Article Sources and Contributors | 117 |
| Image Sources, Licenses and Contributors | 118 |

A

Abbey of Thelema

Thelema Category:Thelema

Core topics

The Book of the Law
Aleister Crowley
True Will · 93
Magick

Mysticism

Thelemic mysticism
The Great Work
Holy Guardian Angel
The Gnostic Mass

Thelemic texts

Works of Crowley
The Holy Books
Thelemite texts

Organizations

A∴A∴ · EGC · OTO
OSOGD · TO

Deities

Nuit · Hadit · Horus
Babalon · Chaos
Baphomet · Choronzon
Ankh-f-n-khonsu
Aiwass · Ma'at

Other topics

Stele of Revealing
Abrahadabra
Unicursal Hexagram
Abramelin oil
Thoth tarot deck

The **Abbey of Thelema** refers to a small house which was used as a temple and spiritual centre founded by Aleister Crowley and Leah Hirsig in Cefalù, Sicily in 1920.

The name was borrowed from François Rabelais's satire *Gargantua and Pantagruel*, where an *Abbey of Theleme* is described as a sort of "anti-monastery" where the lives of the inhabitants were "spent not in laws, statutes, or rules, but according to their own free will and pleasure." This idealistic utopia was to be the model of Crowley's commune, while also being a type of magical school, giving it the designation "Collegium ad Spiritum Sanctum", The College of the Holy Spirit. The general programme was in line with the A∴A∴ course of training, and included daily adorations to the sun, a study of Crowley's writings, regular yogic and ritual practices (which were to be recorded), as well as general domestic labor. The object was for students to devote themselves to the Great Work of discovering and manifesting their True Will.[citation needed]

Crowley had planned to transform the small house into a global center of magical devotion and perhaps to gain tuition fees paid by acolytes seeking training in the Magical Arts; these fees would further assist him in his efforts to promulgate Thelema and publish his manuscripts.[citation needed]

Two women, Hirsig and Shumway (her magical name was Sister Cypris after Aphrodite), were both carrying Crowley's seed. Hirsig had a two-year old son named Hansi and Shumway had a three-year old boy named Howard; they were not Crowley's but he nicknamed them Dionysus and Hermes respectively. After Hirsig's Poupée died, Hirsig had a miscarriage but Shumway gave birth to a daughter (11/12/20), Astarte Lulu Panthea. Astarte was raised in the USA from 1931 by Ninette's older sister Helene Fraux. Astarte has four children including jazz painist Eric Muhler.

Hirsig suspected Shumway's Black Magic foul play and what Crowley found when reading Shumway's magical diary (everybody had to keep one while at the abbey for reasons explained in Liber E) appalled him. Shumway was banished from the abbey and the Beast lamented the death of his children. However, Shumway was soon back in the abbey again to take care of her offspring.

Raoul Loveday

In 1923, a 23-year-old Oxford undergraduate by the name of Raoul Loveday (or Frederick Charles Loveday) died at the Abbey. His wife, Betty May, variously blamed the death on his participation in one of Crowley's rituals (allegedly incorporating the consumption of the blood of a sacrificed cat) or the more probable diagnosis of acute enteric fever contracted by drinking from a mountain spring. (Crowley had warned the couple against drinking the water, as reported in biographies by Lawrence Sutin, Richard Kaczynski and others.) When May returned to London, she gave an interview to a tabloid paper, *The Sunday Express*, which included her story in its ongoing attacks on Crowley. With these and similar rumors about activities at the Abbey in mind, Benito Mussolini's government demanded that Crowley leave the country in 1923. After Crowley's departure, the Abbey of Thelema was eventually abandoned and local residents whitewashed over Crowley's murals.

Current status and popular culture

The villa still stands today, but in poor condition. Filmmaker Kenneth Anger, himself a devotee of Crowley, later uncovered and filmed some of its murals in his film *Thelema Abbey* (1955) now considered a lost film. Recently other murals were uncovered, and pictures of them were posted on the Internet. "Abbey of Thelema" remains a popular name for various magical societies, Witchcraft covens, and Satanist grottoes. It is also the name of a fan club for controversial rock star Marilyn Manson, who included the line "We're gonna ride to the Abbey of Thelema, to the Abbey of Thelema..." in his song "Misery Machine". Experimental musicians Coil, known to be fascinated by mysticism, went a step further in "The Sea Priestess" on *Astral Disaster*, whose lyrics are a bizarre interpretation of the murals in the Abbey.[citation needed]

Notes

The Abbey is currently for sale. Kenneth Anger revisited the Abbey in 2007, 52 years after his 1955 visit, and made a short video which can be found as an "extra" on the "Anger Me" DVD

External links

- Thélema Abbey - Official website from Sicily [1]
- Photos of the Abbey from 2005 [2]
- Abbey of Thelema movie on IMDB [3]

Abramelin oil

Abramelin oil, also called **Oil of Abramelin**, is a ceremonial magical oil blended from aromatic plant materials. Its name came about due to its having been described in a medieval grimoire called *The Book of Abramelin* written by Abraham the Jew. The recipe is adapted from the Jewish Holy anointing oil of the Tanakh, which is described in the Book of Exodus attributed to Moses.

Abramelin oil became popular in the Western esoteric tradition in the 20th century after the publication of the S. L. MacGregor Mathers English translation of the Book of Abramelin, and especially via Aleister Crowley, who used a similar version of the oil in his system of Magick. There are multiple recipes in use today and the oil continues to be used in several modern occult traditions, particularly Thelema and the Ecclesia Gnostica Catholica.

Ingredients and methods of preparation

There are, especially among English-speaking occultists, numerous variant forms of Abramelin Oil.

Abramelin oil

In the English translation by Steven Guth of Georg Dehn's edition, which was compiled from all the known German manuscript sources, the formula reads as follows:

> Take one part of the best myrrh, half a part of cinnamon, one part of cassia, one part galanga root, and a quarter of the combined total weight of good, fresh olive oil. Make these into an ointment or oil as is done by the chemists. Keep it in a clean container until you need it. Put the container together with the other accessories in the cupboard under the altar.

Guth's translation of the recipe may be incorrect. The German sources clearly list "Calmus" or "Kalmus". Guth has translated these as "galanga root". Taking this into account, the five ingredients listed by Abraham of Worms in *The Book of Abramelin* are identical to those listed in the Bible. Only the proportions are slightly different (one-half versus one part of calamus).

In the first printed edition, Peter Hammer, 1725, the recipe reads:

> Nimm Mhrrhen des besten 1 Theil, Zimmt 1/2 Theil, soviel des Calmus als Zimmet, Cassien soviel als der Myrrhen im Gewicht und gutes frisches Baumöl..." (Take 1 part of the best myrrh, 1/2 part cinnamon, as much calamus as cinnamon, of cassia as much as the myrrh in weight and good fresh tree oil...)

Note that the proportions in this edition have been changed to conform with the recipe for Holy anointing oil from the Bible:

> Take thou also unto thee principal spices, of pure myrrh five hundred [shekels], and of sweet cinnamon half so much, [even] two hundred and fifty [shekels], and of sweet calamus two

hundred and fifty [shekels], And of cassia five hundred [shekels], after the shekel of the sanctuary, and of oil olive an hin: And thou shalt make it an oil of holy ointment, an ointment compounded after the art of the apothecary: it shall be an holy anointing oil.

Samuel Mathers' Abramelin oil

According to the S.L. MacGregor Mathers English translation, which derives from an incomplete French manuscript copy of the book, the recipe is:

> You shall prepare the sacred oil in this manner: Take of myrrh in tears, one part; of fine cinnamon, two parts; of galangal half a part; and the half of the total weight of these drugs of the best oil olive. The which aromatics you shall mix together according unto the art of the apothecary, and shall make thereof a balsam, the which you shall keep in a glass vial which you shall put within the cupboard (formed by the interior) of the altar.

The four ingredients listed by Mathers in his translation of *The Book of the Sacred Magic of Abramelin the Mage* are Myrrh, Cinnamon, Galangal, and Olive oil. The word that he translated from the French as "Galangal" is actually the word "Calamus." The other extant manuscripts also list "Calamus" as the ingredient. It is unknown if Mathers' use of Galangal instead of Calamus was intentional or a mistranslation, but it was to result in several notable changes, including symbolism and use.

Since Cinnamon and Cassia are two species of the same Cinnamomum genus, their doubling up into one name by the translator of the French manuscript is not unexpected. His reasons for doing so may have been prompted by a pious decision to avoid duplicating true Holy Oil, or by a tacit admission that in medieval Europe, it was difficult to obtain Cinnamon and Cassia as separate products.

Abramelin oil made with essential oils

A recipe for Abramelin oil using essential oils is as follows:

- half part Cinnamon essential oil
- 1 parts Myrrh essential oil
- 1 part Calamus essential oil
- 1 part Cassia essential oil
- one-quarter of the foregoing total weight Olive oil

Since ancient perfumers and apothecaries never compounded their fragrances by mixing essential oils in such large ratio with respect to carrier oils—because the original formula was to be distilled after maceration, not before—it is possible to restore the proportions to something like what they might have been if maceration and distillation had occurred "according to the art of the apothecary":

- half part Cinnamon essential oil
- 1 parts Myrrh essential oil
- 1 part Calamus essential oil

- 1 part Cassia essential oil
- 7 parts Olive oil

This is a highly fragranced oil that may be applied to the skin in more liberal amounts; it is a close, modern approximation of the oil described by Abramelin to Abraham of Worms.

Macerated Abramelin oil

A recipe for Abramelin oil based upon the French manuscript:

- 4 parts Cinnamon bark quills, reduced to powder
- 2 parts Myrrh resin, finely ground
- 1 part Calamus chopped root, reduced to powder
- half of the foregoing total weight Olive oil

The mixture is macerated for one month, then decanted and bottled for use, producing a fragranced oil suitable for anointing any portion of the body, and will not burn the skin. It may be applied liberally, after the manner of traditional Jewish Holy Oils, such as the one which was poured on Aaron's head until it ran down his beard. It is not, however, made "according unto the art of the apothecary", since it is not distilled after the maceration but decanted into bottles.

Mathers' Macerated Abramelin oil

Making Abramelin oil according to Mathers' translation of the French manuscript requires compounding the oil from raw ingredients. The ratio given in the book is as follows:

- 4 parts Cinnamon bark quills, reduced to powder
- 2 parts Myrrh resin tears, finely ground
- 1 part Galangal sliced root, reduced to powder
- half of the foregoing total weight Olive oil

This mixture is macerated for one month, and then using an apothecary's perfume press the oil would then be separated and bottled for use. The result is a fragranced oil suitable for anointing any portion of the body, and it will not burn the skin.

As essential oils are approximately 2% of raw ingredients on average, it is possible to make the oil this way using essential oils, by multiplying the total weight by 25 [50 for total weight, divided by 2] for the olive oil quantity or enough olive oil to ensure that the essential oils are completely dissolved. This will have the same effect of the oil no longer burning the skin. Once dissolved the olive oil will change from green to silver in colour.

Crowley's Abramelin oil made with essential oils

Early in the 20th century, the British occultist Aleister Crowley created his own version of Abramelin Oil, which he called "Oil of Abramelin," and sometimes referred to as the "Holy Oil of Aspiration." It was based on Mathers' substitution of Galangal for Calamus. Crowley also abandoned the book's method of preparation—which specifies blending Myrrh "tears" (resin) and "fine" (finely ground) Cinnamon—instead opting for pouring together distilled essential oils with a small amount of olive oil. His recipe (from his Commentary to Liber Legis [1]) reads as follows:

- 8 parts Cinnamon essential oil
- 4 parts Myrrh essential oil
- 2 parts Galangal essential oil
- 7 parts Olive oil

Crowley weighed out his proportions of essential oils according to the recipe specified by Mathers' translation for weighing out raw materials. The result is to give the Cinnamon a strong presence, so that when it is placed upon the skin "it should burn and thrill through the body with an intensity as of fire." This formula is unlike the grimoire recipe and it cannot be used for practices that require the oil to be poured over the head. Rather, Crowley intended it to be applied in small amounts, usually to the top of the head or the forehead, and to be used for anointment of magical equipment as an act of consecration.

Doubly-consecrated Crowley oil of Abramelin recipe

It is possible to add 1 part of a previously consecrated batch of the Crowley version of Abramelin oil to each new batch. This can be done for magical reasons and does not change the proportions of the ingredients.

Symbolism of the ingredients

Many traditions of magic work with plant materials, and most also assign some symbolic meanings or ascriptions to these ingredients.

In the Jewish tradition, from whence came the original Biblical recipe upon which Abramelin Oil is based, the Olive is a symbol of domestic felicity and stability, Myrrh (which contains opioids) is believed to be sacred to the Lord, Calamus is known for its sweetness and phalliform fruiting body and stands for fertility and for love, while Cinnamon is favoured for its warming ability.

In hoodoo folk magic, these symbolisms are somewhat changed: Myrrh and Olive remain the same, but Cinnamon is for money and luck, and Calamus is used to sweetly control others. (The Matherian alternative, Galangal, is employed in protective work, especially that involving court cases.)

Crowley also had a symbolic view of the ingredients that he found in the Mathers translation:

> This oil is compounded of four substances. The basis of all is the oil of the olive. The olive is, traditionally, the gift of Minerva, the Wisdom of God, the Logos. In this are dissolved three other

oils; oil of myrrh, oil of cinnamon, oil of galangal. The Myrrh is attributed to Binah, the Great Mother, who is both the understanding of the Magician and that sorrow and compassion which results from the contemplation of the Universe. The Cinnamon represents Tiphereth, the Sun -- the Son, in whom Glory and Suffering are identical. The Galangal represents both Kether and Malkuth, the First and the Last, the One and the Many, since in this Oil they are One. [...] These oils taken together represent therefore the whole Tree of Life. The ten Sephiroth are blended into the perfect gold.

Abramelin oil in occult tradition

The original popularity of Abramelin Oil rested on the importance magicians place upon Jewish traditions of Holy Oils and, more recently, upon Mathers' translation of *The Book of the Sacred Magic of Abramelin the Mage* and the resurgence of 20th century occultism, such as found in the works of the Hermetic Order of the Golden Dawn and Aleister Crowley, and has since spread into other modern occult traditions.

Because it derives from the formula for Jewish Holy Oil, Abramelin Oil also finds use among Jewish and Christian Kabbalists who are not specifically performing the works described by Abraham of Worms. However, the oil can be used in the course of ritual activities outlined in the book by Abramelin the Mage in order to obtain the outcomes he promised those who successfully applied his system of "Divine Science" and "True Magic", namely, the gifts of flight, treasure-finding, and invisibility, as well as the power to cast effective love spells.

Oil of Abramelin and Thelema

Oil of Abramelin was seen as highly important by Aleister Crowley, the founder of Thelema, and he used his version of it throughout his life. In Crowley's mystical system, the oil came to symbolize the aspiration to what he called the Great Work—"The oil consecrates everything that is touched with it; it is his aspiration; all acts performed in accordance with that are holy." [2]

Crowley went on to say

> The Holy Oil is the Aspiration of the Magician; it is that which consecrates him to the performance of the Great Work; and such is its efficacy that it also consecrates all the furniture of the Temple and the instruments thereof. It is also the grace or chrism; for this aspiration is not ambition; it is a quality bestowed from above. For this reason the Magician will anoint first the top of his head before proceeding to consecrate the lower centres in their turn (...) It is the pure light translated into terms of desire. It is not the Will of the Magician, the desire of the lower to reach the higher; but it is that spark of the higher in the Magician which wishes to unite the lower with itself.

This oil is currently used in several ceremonies of the Thelemic church, Ecclesia Gnostica Catholica, including the rites of Baptism, Confirmation, and Ordination. It is also commonly used to consecrate magical implements and temple furniture. The eucharistic host of the Gnostic Mass—called the Cake of Light—includes this oil as an important ingredient.

Effects of Mathers' recipe and Crowley's use of essential oils

Mathers' use of the ingredient galangal instead of calamus and/or Crowley's innovative use of essential oils rather than raw ingredients has resulted in some interesting changes from the original recipe:

- **Scent**: The oils of Mathers and Crowley have a different aroma from the Jewish Abramelin oil. The scent of galangal is gingery and spicy whereas calamus is florally sweet yet a bit yeasty—although the scent of the final oil is strongly cinnamon.
- **Symbolism**: In Jewish, Greek, and European magical botanic symbolism, the ascription given to sweet flag or calamus is generally that of fertility, due to the shape of the plant's fruiting body. Crowley gave the following Qabalistic meaning for galangal: "Galangal represents both Kether and Malkuth, the First and the Last, the One and the Many." Thus Crowley's substitution therefore shifts the symbolism to microcosm/macrocosm unity, which is reflective of Thelema's mystical aim—the union of the adept with the Absolute.
- **Skin sensation**: The original recipe for Abramelin Oil does not irritate the skin and can be applied according to traditional Jewish and Christian religious and magical practices. Crowley's recipe has a much higher concentration of cinnamon than the original recipe. This results in an oil which can be noticeably hot on the skin and can cause skin rashes if applied too liberally.
- **Digestive toxicity**: Galangal is edible, calamus is not, as it has some toxicity. This is certainly relevant to those who use Crowley's Oil of Abramelin as a core ingredient for the eucharistic Cake of Light, giving it a mild opiated taste (from the myrrh) and a spicy tang (from the cinnamon and the ginger-like galangal). Heavy use of calamus in such a recipe would render the host inedible.

See also

- Holy anointing oil
- Holy Guardian Angel
- Magick
- Mysticism
- List of magical terms and traditions

References

- Abraham von Worms, edited by Beecken, Johann Richard. (1957).*Die heilige Magie des Abramelin von Abraham.* ISBN 3-87702-017-8
- Abraham von Worms, edited by Dehn, Georg. *Buch Abramelin das ist Die egyptischen großen Offenbarungen. Oder des Abraham von Worms Buch der wahren Praktik in der uralten göttlichen Magie.* (Editions Araki, 2001) ISBN 3-936149-00-3
- Abraham of Worms, edited by Dehn, Georg. *Book of Abramelin: A New Translation.* (Nicholas Hays, September 2006) ISBN 0-89254-127-X
- Abraham of Worms, translated and edited by Mathers, S.L. MacGregor. *The Book of the Sacred Magic of Abramelin the Mage.* (1897; reprinted by Dover Publications, 1975) ISBN 0-85030-255-2
- Abraham of Worms, edited by von Inns, Juerg. *Das Buch der wahren Praktik in der goettlichen Magie.* Diederichs Gelbe Reihe. (1988).
- Crowley, Aleister. *Magick: Book 4.* 2nd ed. York Beach, Me. : S. Weiser, 1997.
- Koenig, Peter R. (1995). *Abramelin & Co.* Hiram-Edition. ISBN 3-927890-24-3
- Tisserand, Robert & Balacs, Tony. (1995). "Essential Oil Safety: A Guide for Health Care Professionals" ISBN 0-443-05260-3

External links

- The Anal-retentive's Guide to Oil of Abramelin by Frater RIKB [3]
- Recipe for Mathers-style Macerated Oil of Abramelin by Alchemy Works [4]
- Historical and critical background to the new translation by Georg Dehn, with information about Abraham of Worms [5]
- Thelemic Consecration of the Oil, by T. Apiryon [6]
- Safety Guidelines for Essential Oils [7]

Adept

An **adept** is an individual identified as having attained a specific level of knowledge, skill, or aptitude in doctrines relevant to a particular author or organization.

Authors

H. P. Blavatsky

Although Madame Blavatsky makes liberal use of the term *adept* in her works to refer to any caretaker of ancient occult knowledge, in her 1877 work *Isis Unveiled* she asserts the capabilities of the adept as being able to take active control of elemental spirits as well as the physical and astral conditions of non-adepts.

Alice Bailey

In Alice Bailey's body of writing she outlines a hierarchy of spiritual evolution and an initiatory path along which an individual may choose to advance. In her works an Adept is defined as a being who has taken five of the seven initiations.

Orders

Various occult organizations have steps in which an initiate may ascend in their own magical system. Some call these steps degrees or grades.

Hermetic Order of the Golden Dawn

In the initiatory system of the Hermetic Order of the Golden Dawn, an adept is one who has taken the oath of the 5=6 grade and has been granted the title Adeptus Minor. Symbolically this degree represents a spiritual aspirant who, having mastered the union of the four elements under an upright and balanced spirit, is allowed passage from the *Portal of the Vault of the Adepti* into the tomb of Christian Rosenkreutz in the center of the Rosicrucian Mountain of Initiation, Abiegnus, at the center of the universe. The grade of Adeptus Minor and subsequent grades, Adeptus Major, and Adeptus Exemptus form the Second Order of the Golden Dawn, also called the Rosæ Rubeæ et Aureæ Crucis (The Ruby Rose and Golden Cross). These grades correspond to the kabbalistic sephirah of Tiphereth, Geburah, and Chesed respectively.

The oath of the Adeptus Minor includes a provision to "unite myself with my higher and Divine Genius", a process which is more commonly referred to (by way of Aleister Crowley) as Knowledge and Conversation of the Holy Guardian Angel. To undertake this process the Adeptus Minor must reconfirm the work of earlier grades (Zelator through Philosophus) with their newfound knowledge before passing to the Adeptus Major degree, as a full-fledged adept.

A∴A∴

Aleister Crowley, who formed the A∴A∴, restructured the Golden Dawn system. This system still holds to three forms of adept.

- Student
- Probationer—The Order of the Golden Dawn--
- Neophyte
- Zelator
- Practicus
- Philosophus
- Dominus Liminis—The order of the RC (Rose Cross)--
- Adeptus Minor
- Adeptus Major
- Adeptus Exemptus
- Babe of the Abyss—The Order of the S. S. (Silver Star)--
- Magister Templi
- Magus
- Ipsissimus

Temple of Set

The Temple of Set calls their steps degrees, and places adept second.[citation needed] Its system is as follows:

- Setian (First Degree)
- Adept (Second Degree)
- Priest / Priestess (Third Degree)
- Magister / Magistra Templi (Fourth Degree)
- Magus / Maga (Fifth Degree)
- Ipsissimus / Ipsissima (Sixth Degree)

Illuminates of Thanateros

Also distinguished as degrees, the Illuminates of Thanateros, is a newer style of magic called chaos magic, which places adept closer to the top of their system.[citation needed]

- 4° Neophyte
- 3° Initiate
- 2° Adept
- 1° Magus

Ceremonial magic and theurgic practices

Those who practice esoteric arts such as theurgy, goetia, and Kabbalah are familiar with the word "adept". In the traditions of esoteric Christianity and ritual magic, an adept is one who is skilled or profound, but not a master in these arts.

See also

- *Apprentice Adept*, a series of fantasy/science fiction novels by Piers Anthony
- Initiation
- Mystery cult
- Rosicrucianism
- Western esotericism

References

- Bailey, Alice A.: *Initiation Human and Solar*. New York: Lucis Publishing Company, 1997. ISBN 0-85330-110-7
- Blavatsky, H. P.: *Isis Unveiled*. Theosophical University Press, 1998. ISBN 0-911500-03-0
- Eshelman, James A.: *The Mystical & Magical System of the A∴A∴*. Los Angeles: College of Thelema, 2000. ISBN 0-9704496-0-7
- Leadbeater, Charles W.: *The Inner Life*. The Theosophical Publishing House, 1978. ISBN 0-8356-0502-7
- Regardie, Israel: *The Complete Golden Dawn System of Magic*. Scottsdale, AZ, USA: Falcon Press, 1984. ISBN 0-94140412-9
- http://www.vampiretemple.com

External links

- Golden Dawn FAQ [1]

Akashic records

The **akashic records** (akasha is a Sanskrit word meaning "sky", "space" or "aether") is a term used in theosophy (and Anthroposophy) to describe a compendium of mystical knowledge encoded in a non-physical plane of existence. These records are described as containing all knowledge of human experience and the history of the cosmos. They are metaphorically described as a library; other analogies commonly found in discourse on the subject include a "universal supercomputer" and the "Mind of God". People who describe the records assert that they are constantly updated automatically and that they can be accessed through astral projection or when someone is placed under deep hypnosis. The concept was popularized in the theosophical movements of the 19th century and is derived from Hindu philosophy of Samkhya. It is promulgated in the Samkhya philosophy that the Akashic records are automatically recorded in the atoms of *akasha* ("air" or "aether"), one of the five types of atoms visualized as existing in the atomic theory of Ancient India. The term *akashic records* is frequently used in New Age discourse.

Specific accounts

In his books *Journey of Souls* and *Destiny of Souls, Evidence of Life between Lives*, Michael Newton, a hypnotherapist who has worked with subjects in deep states, has many accounts of the akashic record, or "Book of Life". Souls prior to being incarnated go to a 'library' and view the pages associated with the life they are considering. The pages are not necessarily sequential. Although there may be definitive way points along the course of our lives, our free will can change paths, events and outcomes. As the soul prepares for a life with the intent of learning a particular lesson or satisfying a karmic debt, the soul will also choose a family and a body that will help them with the lessons for this incarnation. For many, some of those images survive "birth amnesia" and become our intuition serving them during their lives.

C.W. Leadbeater, who claimed to be clairvoyant, conducted research into the akashic records. He said he inspected them at the Theosophical Society headquarters in Adyar (Tamil Nadu), India during the summer of 1910 and recorded the results in his book *Man: How, Whence, and Whither?* The book records the history of Atlantis and other civilizations and the future society of Earth in the 28th century.

In *The Law of One, Book I*, a book purported to contain conversations with a channeled "social memory complex" known to humans as "Ra," when the questioner asks where Edgar Cayce received his information, the answer received is, "We have explained before that the intelligent infinity is brought into intelligent energy from eighth density or octave. The one sound vibratory complex called Edgar used this gateway to view the present, which is *not the continuum you experience but the potential social memory complex of this planetary sphere*. The term your peoples have used for this is the "Akashic Record" or the "Hall of Records."

"Future Life Reading" - Helen Stewart Wambach, Ph.D (1925–1985), who lived in Concord, California, claimed to be able to read the akashic record. She said she could hypnotize people and enable them to experience their possible *future* lives in various alternate universes.

Akashic records in popular culture

In June 1976, Thea Alexander published a science fiction novel called *2150 AD* that pictures a future society that has supercomputers capable of routinely accessing the akashic records. People can see scenes from their past lives displayed on video screens attached to the supercomputers.

The manga series *Kanna* features a storyline about a parallel universe. The main characters unearth a "mokkan" (a wooden tablet) written in an ancient language, though not Sanskrit. Once translated by one of the characters, it turns out to be the akashic records. The concept is described in great detail, with the crucial plot point being that the actual events begin to diverge from the written about twenty years before present day.

The television series Eureka features a story arc involving "The Artifact", supposedly a relic from the universe which existed before the Big Bang, which served as an antenna for the Akashic Field.

The anime series Outlaw Star, the Galactic Leyline holds similar properties to that of the Akashic records, in that it records all, and holds the advance knowledge of a forgotten race. Access to the Leyline can allow one to use it as a God Machine, altering fate, cause and effect to change the reality as it is known.

In Type-Moon series such as Fate/Stay Night, a Magi's ultimate goal and their family line's is to seek Akasha, Akashic record. The root of all things, storing all events, realities and possibilities while existing outside of time. Also in Tsukihime Roa, nicknamed the Serpent of Akasha due to his ability to reincarnate, where upon death he migrates his knowledge and memories to a preselected new host.

See also
- The Aquarian Gospel of Jesus the Christ
- Esoteric cosmology
- Mindstream
- Store consciousness
- Terma (Buddhism)
- Seth Lloyd
- Edgar Cayce

External links

- *Akashic record* [1] Robert Todd Carroll, *Skeptic's Dictionary*

Alchemy

Alchemy, derived from the Arabic word *al-kimia* (الكیمیاء, ALA-LC: *al-kīmiyā'*), is both a philosophy and an ancient practice focused on the attempt to change base metals into gold, investigating the preparation of the "elixir of longevity", and achieving ultimate wisdom, involving the improvement of the alchemist as well as the making of several substances described as possessing unusual properties. The practical aspect of alchemy can be viewed as a protoscience, having generated the basics of modern inorganic chemistry, namely concerning procedures, equipment and the identification and use of many current substances.

Alchemy has been practiced in ancient Egypt, Mesopotamia (modern Iraq), India, Persia (modern Iran), China, Japan, Korea, the classical Greco-Roman world, the medieval Islamic world, and then medieval Europe up to the 20th century and 21st Century, in a complex network of schools and philosophical systems spanning at least 2,500 years.

Etymology

Main article: Chemistry (etymology)

The word alchemy derives from the Old French *alquimie*, which is from the Medieval Latin *alchimia*, and which is in turn from the Arabic *al-kimia* (الكیمیاء). This term itself is derived from the Ancient Greek *chemeia* (χημεία) with the addition of the Arabic definite article *al-* (ال). It used to be thought that the ancient Greek word was originally derived in its turn from "Chemia" (Χημία), a version of the Egyptian name for Egypt, which was itself based on the Ancient Egyptian word *kēme* (hieroglyphic Khmi, *black earth*, as opposed to desert sand). Some now think that the word originally derived from *chumeia* (χυμεία) meaning "mixture" and referring to pharmaceutical chemistry. With the later rise of alchemy in Alexandria, the word may have been mistakenly thought by ancient writers to derive from Χημία, and thus became spelt as χημεία, and the original meaning forgotten. The question of the etymology of the word alchemy is still open, and recent research indicates that the Egyptian derivation of the word may be valid.

Alchemy as a philosophical and spiritual discipline

Alchemy became known as the *spagyric art* after Greek words meaning *to separate* and *to join together* in the 16th century, the word probably being coined by Paracelsus. Compare this with one of the dictums of Alchemy in Latin: Solve et Coagula— *Separate, and Join Together* (or *"dissolve and coagulate"*).

The best-known goals of the alchemists were the transmutation of common metals into gold (called chrysopoeia) or silver (less well known is plant alchemy, or "spagyric"); the creation of a "panacea", or the elixir of life, a remedy that, it was supposed, would cure all diseases and prolong life indefinitely; and the discovery of a universal solvent. Although these were not the only uses for the discipline, they were the ones most documented and well-known. Certain Hermetic schools argue that the transmutation of lead into gold is analogical for the transmutation of the physical body (Saturn or lead) into (Gold) with the goal of attaining immortality. This is described as Internal Alchemy. Starting with the Middle Ages, Persian and European alchemists invested much effort in the search for the "philosopher's stone", a legendary substance that was believed to be an essential ingredient for either or both of those goals. Pope John XXII issued a bull against alchemical counterfeiting, and the Cistercians banned the practice amongst their members. In 1403, Henry IV of England banned the practice of Alchemy. In the late 14th century, Piers the Ploughman and Chaucer both painted unflattering pictures of Alchemists as thieves and liars. By contrast, Rudolf II, Holy Roman Emperor, in the late 16th century, sponsored various alchemists in their work at his court in Prague.

"Renel the Alchemist", by Sir William Douglas, 1853

Page from alchemic treatise of Ramon Llull, 16th century

It is a popular belief that Alchemists made contributions to the "chemical" industries of the day—ore testing and refining, metalworking, production of gunpowder, ink, dyes, paints, cosmetics, leather tanning, ceramics, glass manufacture, preparation of extracts, liquors, and so on (it seems that the preparation of *aqua vitae*, the "water of life", was a fairly popular "experiment" among European alchemists). Alchemists contributed distillation to Western Europe. The double origin of Alchemy in Greek philosophy as well as in Egyptian and Mesopotamian technology set, from the start, a double approach: the technological, operative one, which Marie-Louise von Franz call extravert, and the mystic, contemplative, psychological one, which von Franz names as introvert. These are not mutually exclusive, but complementary instead, as meditation requires practice in the real world, and conversely.

Several early alchemists, such as Zosimos of Panopolis, are recorded as viewing alchemy as a spiritual discipline, and, in the Middle Ages, metaphysical aspects, substances, physical states, and molecular material processes as mere metaphors for spiritual entities, spiritual states, and, ultimately, transformations. In this sense, the literal meanings of 'Alchemical Formulas' were a blind, hiding their true spiritual philosophy, which being at odds with the Medieval Christian Church was a necessity that could have otherwise led them to the "stake and rack" of the Inquisition under charges of heresy. Thus, both the transmutation of common metals into gold and the universal panacea symbolized evolution from an imperfect, diseased, corruptible, and ephemeral state towards a perfect, healthy, incorruptible, and everlasting state; and the philosopher's stone then represented a mystic key that would make this evolution possible. Applied to the alchemist himself, the twin goal symbolized his evolution from ignorance to enlightenment, and the stone represented a hidden spiritual truth or power that would lead to that goal. In texts that are written according to this view, the cryptic alchemical symbols, diagrams, and textual imagery of late alchemical works typically contain multiple layers of meanings, allegories, and references to other equally cryptic works; and must be laboriously "decoded" in order to discover their true meaning.

In his *Alchemical Catechism*, Paracelsus clearly denotes that his usage of the metals was a symbol:

> Q. When the Philosophers speak of gold and silver, from which they extract their matter, are we to suppose that they refer to the vulgar gold and silver? A. By no means; vulgar silver and gold are dead, while those of the Philosophers are full of life.

Psychology

Alchemical symbolism has been occasionally used by psychologists and philosophers. Carl Jung reexamined alchemical symbolism and theory and began to show the inner meaning of alchemical work as a spiritual path. Alchemical philosophy, symbols and methods have enjoyed something of a renaissance in post-modern contexts.[citation needed]

Jung saw alchemy as a Western proto-psychology dedicated to the achievement of individuation. In his interpretation, alchemy was the vessel by which Gnosticism survived its various purges into the Renaissance, a concept also followed by others such as Stephan A. Hoeller. In this sense, Jung viewed alchemy as comparable to a Yoga of the East, and more adequate to the Western mind than Eastern religions and philosophies. The practice of Alchemy seemed to change the mind and spirit of the Alchemist. Conversely, spontaneous changes on the mind of Western people undergoing any important stage in individuation seems to produce, on occasion, imagery known to Alchemy and relevant to the person's situation.

His interpretation of Chinese alchemical texts in terms of his analytical psychology also served the function of comparing Eastern and Western alchemical imagery and core concepts and hence its possible inner sources (archetypes).

Marie-Louise von Franz, a disciple of Jung, continued Jung's studies on Alchemy and its psychological meaning.

Magnum opus

Main article: Great Work

The Great Work; mystic interpretation of its four stages:

- *nigredo (-putrefactio)*, blackening (-putrefaction): corruption, dissolution, individuation, *see also Suns in alchemy - Sol Niger*
- *albedo*, whitening: purification, burnout of impurity; the moon, female
- *citrinitas*, yellowing: spiritualization, enlightenment; the sun, male;
- *rubedo*, reddening: unification of man with God, unification of the limited with the unlimited.

After the 15th century, many writers tended to compress *citrinitas* into *rubedo* and consider only three stages.

However, it is in citrinitas that the Chemical Wedding takes place, generating the Philosophical Mercury without which the Philosopher's Stone, triumph of the Work, could never be accomplished.

Within the Magnum Opus was the creation of the Sanctae Moleculae, that is the 'Sacred Masses' that were derived from the Sacrae Particulae, that is the 'Sacred Particles', needed to complete the process of achieving the Magnum Opus.[citation needed]

Alchemy as a subject of historical research

The history of alchemy has become a vigorous academic field. As the obscure hermetic language of the alchemists is gradually being "deciphered", historians are becoming more aware of the intellectual connections between that discipline and other facets of Western cultural history, such as the sociology and psychology of the intellectual communities, kabbalism, spiritualism, Rosicrucianism, and other mystic movements, cryptography, witchcraft, and the evolution of science and philosophy.

History

Main article: History of alchemy

See also: Chrysopoeia

Alchemy is the science of understanding, deconstructing, and reconstructing matter, although it is often seen only as the pursuit of turning common metals into gold. A scientific theory says that if Alchemy is stopped in the process of deconstructing, the object will be destroyed. According to Marie-Louise von Franz, the initial basis for alchemy were Egyptian metal technology and mummification, Mesopotamian technology and astrology, and Pre-Socratic Greek philosophers such as Empedocles, Thales of Miletus and Heraclitus.

The origins of Western alchemy are traceable back to ancient Egypt. The Leyden papyrus X and the Stockholm papyrus along with the Greek magical papyri comprise the first "book" on alchemy still existent. Babylonian, Greek, Indian, Chinese, and other philosophers theorized that the complexity of nature can be explained with a small set of elements, such as those of Empedocles: *Earth, Fire, Water,* and *Air*. They have little conceptional similarity to today's 117 chemical elements. In the Middle Ages, Jābir ibn Hayyān's theories and list of seven elements, including sulfur and mercury, were augmented and slowly displaced by more modern criteria for elements and theories of chemistry during the early modern period.

Alchemy encompasses several philosophical traditions spanning four millennia and three continents. These traditions' general penchant for cryptic and symbolic language makes it hard to trace their mutual influences and "genetic" relationships. Alchemy starts becoming much clearer in the 8th century with the works of the Islamic alchemist, Jābir ibn Hayyān (known as "Geber" in Europe), who introduced a methodical and experimental approach to scientific research based in the laboratory, in contrast to the ancient Greek and Egyptian alchemists whose works were mainly allegorical.

Other famous alchemists include Rhazes, Avicenna and Imad ul-din in Persia; Wei Boyang in Chinese alchemy; and Nagarjuna in Indian alchemy; and Albertus Magnus and Pseudo-Geber in European alchemy; as well as the anonymous author of the *Mutus Liber*, published in France in the late 17th century, which was a 'wordless book' that claimed to be a guide to making the philosopher's stone, using a series of 15 symbols and illustrations. The philosopher's stone was an object that was thought to be able to amplify one's power in alchemy and, if possible, grant the user ageless immortality, unless he fell victim to burnings or drowning; the common belief was that fire and water were the two greater elements that were implemented into the creation of the stone.

In the case of the Chinese and European alchemists, there was a difference between the two. The European alchemists tried to transmute lead into gold, and, no matter how futile or toxic the element, would continue trying until it was royally outlawed later into the century. The Chinese, however, paid no heed to the philosopher's stone or transmutation of lead to gold; they focused more on medicine for the greater good. During Enlightenment, these "elixirs" were a strong cure for sicknesses, unless it was a test medicine. In general, most tests were fatal, but stabilized elixirs served great purposes. On the other hand, the Islamic alchemists were interested in alchemy for a variety of reasons, whether it was for the transmutation of metals or artificial creation of life, or for practical uses such as medicine.

During the 17th century, practical Alchemy started to evolve into "Chemistry",[citation needed] as it was renamed by Robert Boyle, the "father of modern Chemistry". In his book, *The Skeptical Chymist*, Boyle attacked Paracelsus and the venerable natural philosophy of Aristotle, which was taught at universities. However, Boyle's biographers, in their emphasis that he laid the foundations of modern chemistry, neglect how steadily he clung to the Scholastic sciences and to Alchemy, in theory, practice and doctrine.

A tentative outline is as follows:

1. Egyptian alchemy [5000 BC – 400 BC], beginning of alchemy
2. Indian alchemy [1200 BC – Present], related to Indian metallurgy; Nagarjuna was an important alchemist
3. Greek alchemy [332 BC – 642 AD], studied at the Library of Alexandria Stockholm papyrus
4. Chinese alchemy [142 AD], Wei Boyang writes *The Kinship of the Three*
5. Islamic alchemy [700 – 1400], Jābir ibn Hayyān develops experimental method for alchemy during the Islamic Golden Age
6. Islamic chemistry [800 – Present], Alkindus and Avicenna refute transmutation, Rhazes refutes four classical elements
7. European alchemy [1300 – Present], Saint Albertus Magnus builds on Islamic alchemy
8. European chemistry [1661 – Present], Boyle writes *The Sceptical Chymist*, Lavoisier writes *Traité Élémentaire de Chimie (Elements of Chemistry)*, and Dalton publishes his *Atomic Theory*

Modern connections to alchemy

Persian alchemy was a forerunner of modern scientific chemistry. Alchemists used many of the same laboratory tools that are used today. These tools were not usually sturdy or in good condition, especially during the medieval period of Europe. Many transmutation attempts failed when alchemists unwittingly made unstable chemicals. This was made worse by the unsafe conditions in which the alchemists worked.

Up to the 16th century, alchemy was considered serious science in Europe; for instance, Isaac Newton devoted considerably more of his writing to the study of alchemy (see Isaac Newton's occult studies) than he did to either optics or physics, for which he is famous. Other eminent alchemists of the Western world are Roger Bacon, Saint Thomas Aquinas, Tycho Brahe, Thomas Browne, and Parmigianino. The decline of alchemy began in the 18th century with the birth of modern chemistry, which provided a more precise and reliable framework for matter transmutations and medicine, within a new grand design of the universe based on rational materialism.

Alchemy in traditional medicine

Traditional medicines involve transmutation by alchemy, using pharmacological or a combination of pharmacological and spiritual techniques. In Chinese medicine the alchemical traditions of pao zhi will transform the nature of the temperature, taste, body part accessed or toxicity. In Ayurveda the samskaras are used to transform heavy metals and toxic herbs in a way that removes their toxicity. These processes are actively used to the present day.

Nuclear transmutation

Main articles: Nuclear transmutation and Synthesis of noble metals

In 1919, Ernest Rutherford used artificial disintegration to convert nitrogen into oxygen. From then on, this sort of *scientific transmutation* has been routinely performed in many nuclear physics-related laboratories and facilities, like particle accelerators, nuclear power stations and nuclear weapons as a by-product of fission and other physical processes.

In literature

Sir Thomas Malory uses Alchemy as a motif that underlies the personal, psychological, and aesthetic development of Sir Gareth of Orkney in Le Morte d'Arthur[citation needed]. Sir Gareth's quest parallels the process of Alchemy in that he first undergoes the *nigredo* phase by defeating the black knight and wearing his armor. After this, Gareth defeats knights representing the four elements, thereby subsuming their power. In fighting and defeating the Red Knight (the overall purpose of his quest) he undergoes and passes the *rubedo* phase. Gareth, toward the end of his quest, accepts a ring from his paramour, Lyoness, which transforms his armor into being multicolored. This alludes to the panchromatic philosopher's stone, and while he is in multicolored armor, he is unbeatable.

A play by Ben Jonson, The Alchemist, is a satirical and skeptical take on the subject.

Part 2 of Goethe's Faust, is full of alchemical symbolism.

According to *Hermetic Fictions: Alchemy and Irony in the Novel* (Keele University Press, 1995), by David Meakin, alchemy is also featured in such novels and poems as those by William Godwin, Percy Bysshe Shelley, Emile Zola, Jules Verne, Marcel Proust, Thomas Mann, Hermann Hesse, James Joyce, Gustav Meyrink, Lindsay Clarke, Marguerite Yourcenar, Umberto Eco, Michel Butor, Paulo Coelho, Amanda Quick, Gabriel García Marquez and Maria Szepes.

Hilary Mantel, in her novel Fludd (1989, Penguin), mentions the spagyric art. 'After separation, drying out, moistening, dissolving, coagulating, fermenting, comes purification, recombination: the creation of substances the world until now has never beheld. This is the opus contra naturem, this is the spagyric art, this is the Alchymical Wedding'. (page 79)

In Dante's Inferno, it is placed within the Tenth ring of the 8th circle.

In *Harry Potter and the Philosopher's Stone*, there are several references to Nicholas Flamel, and a stone that could turn metal into gold and create an elixir of immortality was sought after by both the villains and Harry and friends, for different reasons.

The manga and anime series Fullmetal Alchemist bases itself on a more fantasised version of alchemy, based on the principle of equivalent exchange. In the manga and anime series Buso Renkin, alchemy is used to form Kakugane, which transforms into a weapon based on a human's fighting instincts. Also, alchemy is used to create homunculi.

The main character in the play Goodnight Desdemona (Good Morning Juliet), by Ann-Marie MacDonald, attempts (and succeeds) at determining the alchemy behind Shakespeare's work, Othello.

In contemporary art

In the twentieth century alchemy was a profoundly important source of inspiration for the Surrealist artist Max Ernst, who used the symbolism of alchemy to inform and guide his work. M.E. Warlick wrote his *Max Ernst and Alchemy* describing this relationship in detail.

Contemporary artists use alchemy as inspiring subject matter, like Odd Nerdrum, whose interest has been noted by Richard Vine, and the painter Michael Pearce, whose interest in alchemy dominates his work. His works *Fama* and *The Aviator's Dream* particularly express alchemical ideas in a painted allegory.

See also

- Outline of Alchemy

References

- Cavendish, Richard, The Black Arts, Perigee Books
- Gettgins, Fred (1986). *Encyclopedia of the Occult*. London: Rider.
- Greenberg, Adele Droblas (2000). *Chemical History Tour, Picturing Chemistry from Alchemy to Modern Molecular Science*. Wiley-Interscience. ISBN 0-471-35408-2.
- Hart-Davis, Adam (2003). *Why does a ball bounce? 101 Questions that you never thought of asking*. New York: Firefly Books.
- Hughes, Jonathan (2002). *Arthurian Myths and Alchemy, the Kingship of Edward IV*. Stroud: Sutton. ISBN 0750919949.
- Marius (1976). *On the Elements*. Berkeley: University of California Press. ISBN 0-520-02856-2. Trans. Richard Dales.
- Thorndike, Lynn (1923-1958) (8 volumes). *A History of Magic and Experimental Science*. New York: Macmillan. ISBN 0231087942.

- Weaver, Jefferson Hane (1987). *The World of Physics*. New York: Simon & Schuster. ISBN 0306430762.
- Zumdahl, Steven S. (1989). *Chemistry* (2nd ed.). Lexington, Maryland: D.C. Heath and Company. ISBN 0-669-16708-8.
- Halleux, R., *Les textes alchimiques*, Brepols Publishers, 1979, ISBN 978-2-503-36032-4

External links

- Alchemy [1] on In Our Time at the BBC. (listen now [2])
- Etymology of "alchemy" [3]
- Hidden Symbolism of Alchemy and the Occult Arts [4] by Herbert Silberer
- The Alchemy website [5] - Alchemy from a metaphysical perspective.
- The al-kemi.org website [6] - Alchemy from a spiritual/philosophical perspective.
- Society for the History of Alchemy and Chemistry [7]
- Alchemy images [8]
- *Dictionary of the History of Ideas*: [9] Alchemy
- *Antiquity*, Vol. 77 (2003) [10] - "A 16th century lab in a 21st century lab".
- The Story of Alchemy and the Beginnings of Chemistry [11], Muir, M. M. Pattison (1913)
- "Transforming the Alchemists" [12], New York Times, August 1, 2006. Historical revisionism and alchemy.
- Electronic library [13] with hundreds of alchemical books (15th- and 20th century) and 160 original manuscripts.
- The Chymistry of Isaac Newton [14] - A scholarly site devoted to the alchemical, or chymical, writings of Isaac Newton.
- Rex Research [15] - Numerous online alchemical texts.

Ascended master

Ascended Masters, in the Ascended Master Teachings is derived from the Theosophical concept of Masters of the Ancient Wisdom or "Mahatmas". They are believed to be spiritually enlightened beings who in past incarnations were ordinary humans, but who have undergone a process of spiritual transformation. The term "Ascended Master" was first introduced in 1934 with the publication of *Unveiled Mysteries* by Guy Ballard in The "I AM" Activity. This concept was further popularized by authors such as Baird T. Spalding during the 1930s, and in books like The Bridge to Freedom (1951), The Summit Lighthouse (1958), and various other organizations such as the White Eagle Lodge (1936).

Beliefs about Ascended Masters

Originally presented by H. P. Blavatsky in the 1870s, the "Masters of Wisdom" or "Mahatmas" or "Elder Brothers" were further developed by C. W. Leadbeater, Alice Bailey, Helena Roerich, Manly P. Hall. Later on many others in theosophy-based organizations, especially in the United States, developed the concept of Ascended Masters which departs from the theosophical one in several aspects. It is believed that Ascended Masters are individuals who were formerly embodied on the Earth and learned the lessons of life during their incarnations. They gained mastery over the limitations of the matter planes, balanced at least 51% of negative karma, and fulfilled their Dharma (Divine Plan). An Ascended Master, in such an understanding, has become God-like and a source of unconditional "Divine Love" to all life, and through the Ascension has united with his or her own "God Self," the "I AM Presence."

It is further claimed by various groups and teachers that the Ascended Masters serve as the teachers of mankind from the realms of Spirit, and that all people will eventually attain their Ascension and move forward in spiritual evolution beyond this planet. According to these teachings, they remain attentive to the spiritual needs of humanity, and act to inspire and motivate its spiritual growth. In many traditions and organizations, they are considered part of the *Spiritual Hierarchy for Earth*, and members of the *Great Brotherhood of Light*, also known as the *Great White Lodge, Great White Brotherhood,* or *Universal White Brotherhood* (per Peter Deunov).

According to Alice Bailey and Benjamin Creme there are sixty *Masters of the Ancient Wisdom*, defined as beings who have reached the Fifth Level of Initiation or above, with Djwhal Khul in a pivotal role as the master who telepathically dictated the many esoteric teachings in Baileys' books. Elizabeth Clare Prophet revealed the names of a number of these Ascended Masters that were previously unknown.

The concept of recognizing the spiritual self, one's own psychological and karma battles and how to overcome them, and eventual Ascension of all humanity is covered in James Redfield's Celestine Prophecy and its sequels, The Tenth Insight: Holding the Vision and The Secret of Shambhala: In Search of the Eleventh Insight. These books, while controversial, are recent popularizations of the concept of Ascension.

Origins

The founder of the Theosophical Society, H. P. Blavatsky, in the late 19th century brought attention to the idea of secret initiatory knowledge, by claiming her ideas were based on traditions transmitted to her by occult means from a group of highly evolved humans which she called the Mahatmas or Masters. These Mahatmas, she claimed, were physical beings living in the Himalayas, usually understood as Tibet.[citation needed]

> ".. they are living men, born as we are born, and doomed to die like every mortal. We call them "masters" because they are our teachers; and because from them we have derived all the Theosophical truths... They are men of great learning, whom we call Initiates, and still greater holiness of life."

While some of her critics believe the Masters are pure fantasy, other writers suggest that her changing stories were meant to hide the identities of real human teachers guiding her work. Blavatsky claimed that she personally met numerous Masters on countless occasions, and was also the guest of the Master Koot Hoomi while visiting the "Little Tibet" region of Kashmir.

After Madame Blavatsky's death in 1891, the Mahatma concept was developed by her successors in the Theosophical Society leadership, Annie Besant and Charles W. Leadbeater, who described the Masters in great detail and added Jesus and Maitreya. In Leadbeater's book, *The Masters and the Path* (1925), the Masters are presented as human beings full of wisdom and compassion, albeit still limited by human bodies. Later theosophy-based organizations developed the theory adding more elements developing the concept of Ascended Masters which bears some important differences with the Theosophical one.[citation needed]

Comparison of unascended and Ascended Masters

There is considerable difference between the concept of Masters of Wisdom in 19th century theosophy (as described by Blavatsky, Olcott, Sinnett, and others) and the current concept of Ascended Masters. The believers in "Immortal Saints and Sages" claim that these individuals have gone through a series of Initiations symbolically represented in the life of Jesus by the stages of Birth, Baptism, Transfiguration, Crucifixion, Resurrection, and the Ascension . The twentieth century teachings of the Ballards, Prophets, and others interpreted these stages as actual events and claim that although Morya and Koot Hoomi (Kuthumi) were Adepts and Masters of the lower matter planes and the elemental forces of nature, they had not become Ascended Masters until 1898, while Serapis and the Maha Chohan, who were interacting with Theosophists during Blavatsky's time, already were Ascended Masters. This is not supported by the original Theosophical view.

An unascended Master has, according to these later teachings, overcome the limitations of the lower matter octaves (physical, emotional, mental), yet has chosen to postpone the final Initiation of the Ascension to remain in time and space to externalize and focus the Consciousness of God for the evolutions of the Earth. If a person takes a Bodhisattva vow, they may choose to remain with the humanity of this Earth as an unascended Master in one of the lower Spirit/Matter Octaves, as was the case with Babaji. It is believed by proponents of these beliefs that if enough mastery and externalization of the Divine Nature has been developed, such an Adept becomes an Initiate of one of the Brotherhoods or Sisterhoods of Light under the auspices of the Great White Brotherhood. It is claimed that there can be a high degree of attainment within the lower body vehicles of expression (physical, emotional, mental, memory), yet that Adept may still not be Ascended (not primarily expressing through the Higher Bodies).

One such teaching claims that examples of unascended Masters are: Yogananda, Mataji, and Lao-tzu. The belief is that they have un-Ascended bodies that are not flesh and blood of the lowest of the sub-plane substance of the physical octave, but of the "finer matter" that composes the upper etheric sub-planes of the physical octave, as well as the emotional (astral) octave, and the mental octave.

The Great White Brotherhood

Main article: Great White Brotherhood

The Masters are collectively called the "Great White Brotherhood" in Theosophical system. The use of the term "white" refers to their advanced spirituality (i.e., that they have a white colored aura) and has nothing to do with race. Blavatsky described many of the Masters as ethnically Tibetan or Indian (Hindu), not European. She did, however, describe them as being from all cultures and races, such as the "Greek gentleman" known as Hilarion.

Belief in the Brotherhood and the Masters is an essential part of the syncretistic teachings of various organizations that have taken the Theosophical philosophical concepts and added their own elements. Examples of those believed to be Ascended Masters by these organizations are Jesus, Sanat Kumara, Gautama Buddha, Maitreya, Confucius, Lord Lanto (Confucius' historical mentor), Mary the Mother of Jesus, Lady Master Nada, Enoch, Kwan Yin, Saint Germain, and Kuthumi, to name but a few. It is believed that all of these put aside any differences they might have had in their Earthly careers, and unite instead to advance the spiritual well-being of humanity.

See also

- Bodhisattva
- Masters of the Ancient Wisdom
- Levitation
- Telepathy

References

- Braden, Charles S. *These Also Believe* MacMillan Publishing Company 1960 (Reprint 2000). The classic study of minority religions in the United States of America. ISBN 0-02-514360-3
- Cranston, Sylvia. *H. P. B. : The Extraordinary Life & Influence of Helena Blavastsky*. G. P. Putnam's Sons 1993 ISBN 0-9662115-1-0
- Godwin, Joscelyn (1994). *The Theosophical Enlightenment*. SUNY Press. ISBN 0-7914-2152-X
- Hall, Manly P. *The Secret Teachings of All Ages* "An Encyclopedic Outline of Masonic, Hermetic, Qabbalistic and Rosicrucian Symbolical Philosophy Being an Interpretation of the Secret Teachings Concealed within the Rituals, Allegories and Mysteries of all Ages" H.S. Crocker Company, Inc. 1928 (Reprint: Tarcher 2003) ISBN 1-58542-250-9
- Leadbeater, C.W. *The Masters and the Path*. The Theosophical Publishing House 1925 (Reprint: Kessinger Publishing 1997). ISBN 1-56459-686-9
- Partridge, Christopher ed. *New Religions: A Guide: New Religious Movements, Sects and Alternative Spiritualities* Oxford University Press, USA 2004. Describes the Theosophical Society, The I AM Activity, The Bridge to Freedom and The Summit Lighthouse. ISBN 0-19-522042-0
- Saint Germain Foundation. *The History of the "I AM" Activity and Saint Germain Foundation*. Saint Germain Press 2003 ISBN 1-878891-99-5
- King, Godfre Ray. *Unveiled Mysteries*. Saint Germain Press 1934. ISBN 1-878891-00-6
- Saint Germain. *I AM Discourses*. Saint Germain Press 1935. ISBN 1-878891-48-0

External links

- The Saint Germain Foundation [1], Original publisher of Ascended Master Teachings beginning in 1934

Astral projection

Astral projection (or **astral travel**) is an interpretation of any form of out-of-body experience (OBE) that assumes the existence of an "astral body" separate from the physical body and capable of travelling outside it. Astral projection or travel denotes the astral body leaving the physical body to travel in the astral plane.

The idea of astral travel is rooted in common worldwide religious accounts of the afterlife in which the consciousness' or soul's journey or "ascent" is described in such terms as "an...out-of body experience, wherein the spiritual traveller leaves the physical body and travels in his/her subtle body (or dreambody or astral body) into 'higher' realms." It is therefore associated with near death experiences and is also frequently reported as spontaneously experienced in association with sleep and dreams, illness, surgical operations, drug experiences, sleep paralysis and forms of meditation.

"The Separation of the Spirit Body" from *The Secret of the Golden Flower*, a Chinese handbook on alchemy and meditation

It is also sometimes attempted for its own sake, or may be believed to be necessary to, or the result of, some forms of spiritual practice. It may involve "travel to higher realms" called astral planes but is commonly used to describe any sensation of being "out of the body" in the everyday world, even seeing one's body from outside or above. It may be reported in the form of an apparitional experience, a supposed encounter with a doppelgänger, some living person also seen somewhere else at the same time.

Through the 1960s and 70s, surveys reported percentages ranging from 8% to as many as 50% (in certain groups) of respondents who state they had such an experience. The subjective nature of the experience permits explanations that do not rely on the existence of an "astral" body and plane. There is little beyond anecdotal evidence to support the idea that people can actually "leave the body".

Beliefs

The theme is treated in anthropological or ethnographic literature on witchcraft and shamanism, in classical philosophy and in various myths and religious scriptures.

Western philosophies

According to classical, medieval and renaissance Neoplatonism, and later Theosophist and Rosicrucian thought, the astral body is an intermediate body of light linking the rational soul to the physical body while the astral plane is an intermediate world of light between Heaven and Earth, composed of the spheres of the planets and stars. These astral spheres were held to be populated by angels, demons and spirits.

The subtle bodies, and their associated planes of existence, form an essential part of the esoteric systems that deal with astral phenomena. In the neo-platonism of Plotinus, for example, the individual is a microcosm ("small world") of the universe (the macrocosm or "great world"). "The rational soul...is akin to the great Soul of the World" while "the material universe, like the body, is made as a faded image of the Intelligible". Each succeeding plane of manifestation is causal to the next, a world-view called emanationism; "from the One proceeds Intellect, from Intellect Soul, and from Soul - in its lower phase, or Nature - the material universe".

Often these bodies and their planes of existence are depicted as a series of concentric circles or nested spheres, with a separate body traversing each realm. The idea of the astral figured prominently in the work of the nineteenth-century French occultist Eliphas Levi, whence it was adopted by Theosophy and the Golden Dawn magical society.

The Bible

A common belief is that the subtle body is attached to the physical body by means of a psychic silver cord. The final chapter of the Biblical Book of Ecclesiastes is often cited in this respect;

> *"before the silver cord be loosed, or the golden bowl be broken, or the pitcher be shattered at the fountain, or the wheel be broken at the cistern"*

Paul's second letter to the Corinthians (Chapter 12, verse 2) is more generally agreed to refer to the astral planes;

> *"I know a man in Christ, fourteen years ago, (whether in the body I know not, or out of the body I know not, God knows) such a one caught up to the third heaven..."*

This statement gave rise to the *Visio Pauli*, a tract that offers a vision of heaven and hell, a forerunner of visions attributed to Adomnan and Tnugdalus as well as of Dante's *Divine Comedy*.

Ancient Egypt

Similar concepts of "soul" travel appear in various other religious traditions, for example ancient Egyptian teachings present the soul as having the ability to hover outside the physical body in the *ka*, or subtle body.

China

Taoist alchemical practice involves creation of an energy body by breathing meditations, drawing energy into a 'pearl' that is then "circulated". "Xiangzi ... with a drum as his pillow fell fast asleep, snoring and motionless. His primordial spirit, however, went straight into the banquet room and said, "My lords, here I am again." ... When Tuizhi walked ... with the officials to take a look, there really was a Daoist sleeping on the ground and snoring like thunder. Yet inside, in the side room, there was another Daoist beating a fisher drum and singing Daoist songs. The officials all said, "Although there are two different people, their faces and clothes are exactly alike. Clearly he is a divine immortal who can divide his body and appear in several places at once. ..." ... At that moment, the Daoist in the side room came walking out, and the Daoist sleeping on the ground woke up. The two merged into one."

India

The Theosophists also took note of similar ideas (Lin'ga S'ari-ra) found in ancient Hindu scriptures such as the YogaVashishta-Maharamayana of Valmiki. Modern Indians who have offered experiences of astral projection include Paramahansa Yogananda and Osho (Bhagwan Shree Rajneesh)

Japan

In Japanese mythology, an **ikiryō** (生口) (also read *shōryō*, *seirei*, or *ikisudama*) is a manifestation of the soul of a living person separately from their body. Traditionally, if someone holds a sufficient grudge against another person, it is believed that a part or the whole of their soul can temporarily leave their body and appear before the target of their hate in order to curse or otherwise harm them, similar to an evil eye. Souls are also believed to leave a living body when the body is extremely sick or comatose; such *ikiryō* are not malevolent.

The *ikiryō* as illustrated by Toriyama Sekien.

Inuit

In some Inuit groups people with special capabilities are said to travel to (mythological) remote places, and report their experiences and things important to their fellows or the entire community; how to stop bad luck in hunting, cure a sick person etc., things unavailable to people with normal capabilities.

Amazon

The *yaskomo* of the Waiwai is believed to be able to perform a "soul flight" that can serve several functions such as healing, flying to the sky to consult cosmological beings (the moon or the brother of the moon) to get a name for a new-born baby, lying to the cave of *peccaries' mountains* to ask the *father of peccaries* for abundance of game or flying deep down in a river to get the help of other beings.

"Astral" and "etheric"

The expression "astral projection" came to be used in two different ways. For the Golden Dawn and some Theosophists it retained the classical and medieval philosophers' meaning of journeying to other worlds, heavens, hells, the astrological spheres and other imaginal landscapes, but outside these circles the term was increasingly applied to non-physical travel around the physical world.

Though this usage continues to be widespread, the term, "etheric travel", used by some later Theosophists, offers a useful distinction. Some experients say they visit different times and/or places: "etheric", then, is used to represent the sense of being "out of the body" in the physical world, whereas "astral" may connote some alteration in time-perception. Robert Monroe describes the former type of projection as "Locale I" or the "Here-Now", involving people and places that actually exist: Robert Bruce calls it the "Real Time Zone" (RTZ) and describes it as the non-physical dimension-level closest to the physical. This etheric body is usually, though not always, invisible but is often perceived by the experient as connected to the physical body during separation by a "silver cord". Some link "falling" dreams with projection.

According to Max Heindel, the etheric "double" serves as a medium between the astral and physical realms. In his system the ether, also called prana, is the "vital force" that empowers the physical forms to change. From his descriptions it can be inferred that, to him, when one views the physical during an out-of-body experience, one is not technically "in" the astral realm at all.

Other experients may describe a domain that has no parallel to any known physical setting. Environments may be populated or unpopulated, artificial, natural or abstract, and the experience may be beatific, horrific or neutral. A common Theosophical belief is that one may access a compendium of mystical knowledge called the Akashic records. In many accounts the experiencer correlates the astral world with the world of dreams. Some even report seeing other dreamers enacting dream scenarios unaware of their wider environment.

The astral environment may also be divided into *levels* or *sub-planes* by theorists, but here are many different views in various traditions concerning the overall structure of the astral planes: they may include heavens and hells and other after-death spheres, transcendent environments or other less-easily characterized states.

Stephen LaBerge suggested in his 1985 book *Lucid Dreaming* that all such "out-of-body experiences" may represent partially lucid dreams or "misinterpreted dream experiences" in which the sleeper does not fully recognize the situation. "In the dark forest, one may experience a tree as a tiger, but it is still in fact only a tree."

Notable practitioners

Emanuel Swedenborg was one of the first practitioners to write extensively about the out-of-body experience, in his Spiritual Diary (1747–65). French philosopher and novelist Honoré de Balzac's fictional work "Louis Lambert" suggests he may have had some astral or out-of-body experience.

There are many twentieth century publications on astral projection, although only a few remain widely cited. These include Robert Monroe, Oliver Fox, Sylvan Muldoon and Hereward Carrington, and Yram.

Carrington, a psychical researcher, and Muldoon, who professed ease with astral projection, jointly published *The Projection of the Astral Body* in 1929. Techniques they felt facilitated projection included visualizing flying or ascending in an elevator just before going to sleep and trying to regain waking consciousness while in a dream state (lucid dreaming) by habitually recognizing apparent incongruities in one's dream such as a different pattern of wallpaper in one's home. Such recognition, they said, sometimes resulted in the feeling of being outside the physical body and able to look down on it.

Robert Monroe's accounts of journeys to other realms (1971–1994) popularized the term "OBE" and were translated into a large number of languages. Though his books themselves only placed secondary importance on descriptions of method, Monroe also founded an institute dedicated to research, exploration and non-profit dissemination of auditory technology for assisting others in achieving projection and related altered states of consciousness.

Robert Bruce, William Buhlmann and Albert Taylor have discussed their theories and findings on the syndicated show Coast to Coast AM several times. Michael Crichton gives lengthy and detailed explanations and experience of astral projection in his non-fiction book "Travels".

Waldo Vieira, a physician and dentist, claims to have had his first OBE at the age of 9 and has gone on to write numerous articles and over 20 books, including *Projectiology*. Wagner Alegretti, president of and researcher at International Academy of Consciousness, is another out-of-body experiencer, featured on the Discovery Channel en Espanol and New York's New Realities series. Rock singer Marilyn Manson says astral projection helped him throughout the recording of Antichrist Superstar.

"Soul Travel", the belief that when one sleeps, the Soul leaves its body and seeks spiritual lessons in the Soul Planes, or heaven, is a key element in the religion of Eckankar. They believe that there are many different Temples that Souls go to in higher planes to learn their religion.

In occult traditions, practices range from inducing trance states to the mental construction of a second body, called the *Body of Light* in Aleister Crowley's writings, through visualization and controlled breathing, followed by the transfer of consciousness to the secondary body by a mental act of will.

References

- Fock, Niels (1963). *Waiwai. Religion and society of an Amazonian tribe*. Nationalmuseets skrifter, Etnografisk Række (Ethnographical series), VIII. Copenhagen: The National Museum of Denmark.
- Hoppál, Mihály (1975). "Az uráli népek hiedelemvilága és a samanizmus". In Hajdú, Péter (in Hungarian). *Uráli népek. Nyelvrokonaink kultúrája és hagyományai*. Budapest: Corvina Kiadó. pp. 211–233. ISBN 963 13 0900 2. The title means: "Uralic peoples / Culture and traditions of our linguistic relatives"; the chapter means "The belief system of Uralic peoples and the shamanism".
- Hoppál, Mihály (2005) (in Hungarian). *Sámánok Eurázsiában*. Budapest: Akadémiai Kiadó. ISBN 963-05-8295-3 2. The title means "Shamans in Eurasia", the book is written in Hungarian, but it is published also in German, Estonian and Finnish. Site of publisher with short description on the book (in Hungarian) [1]
- Kleivan, Inge; B. Sonne (1985). *Eskimos: Greenland and Canada*. Iconography of religions, section VIII, "Arctic Peoples", fascicle 2. Leiden, The Netherlands: Institute of Religious Iconography • State University Groningen. E.J. Brill. ISBN 90-04-07160-1.
- Merkur, Daniel (1985). *Becoming Half Hidden: Shamanism and Initiation among the Inuit*. : Acta Universitatis Stockholmiensis • Stockholm Studies in Comparative Religion. Stockholm: Almqvist & Wiksell. ISBN 91-22-00752-0.
- Klemp, Harold (2003). *Past Lives, Dreams, and Soul Travel*. Eckankar.. Minneapolis, MN. [Eckankar Web site: http://www.eckankar.org]: Eckankar.

See also

- Soul retrieval
- Aura
- Ketamine
- DMT
- Metaphysics
- Esotericism
- Hypnogogia
- Parapsychology
- Sleep paralysis
- Tattva vision
- Teleportation
- Mediumship
- Yoga Nidra

Further reading

- Barton, Mary E. - *Soul Sight: Projections of Consciousness and Out of Body Epiphanies*. ISBN 978-0-557-02163-5
- Bruce, Robert (1999) - *Astral Dynamics: A NEW Approach to Out-of-Body Experiences*. ISBN 1-57174-143-7
- Buhlman, William - *Adventures Beyond the Body: How to experience out-of-body travel*. ISBN 978-0-06-251371-7
- Leland, Kurt. - *Otherwhere: A Field Guide to Nonphysical Reality for the Out-of-Body Traveler*. Hampton Roads Publishing (2001). ISBN 978-1571742414
- Muldoon, Sylvan J. and Carrington, Hereward - *Projection of the Astral Body*. ISBN 0766146049
- Monroe, Robert - *Journeys Out of the Body* Doubleday (1971). reprinted (1989) Souvenir Press Ltd. ISBN 978-0285627536
- Peterson, Robert - *Out of Body Experiences*. ISBN 1571740570
- Pritchard, Mark H - *A Course in Astral Travel and Dreams*. Absolute Publishing Press (2005). Second edition. ISBN 0974056030
- Stack, Rick - *Out of Body Adventures*. ISBN 0-8092-4560-4
- Vieira, Dr. Waldo - *Projectiology*. ISBN 85-86019-58-5
- Wilde, Stuart - *Sixth Sense*. ISBN 1-56170-501-2

External links

Part of a series of articles on the paranormal
Main articles
Paranormal · Supernatural · Occult · Forteana · Miracle · Magic · Aura · Ghost · Ghost hunting · Ghost story · Fear of ghosts · Poltergeist · Cold spot · Haunted locations: World, United States, United Kingdom · Haunted house · Intelligent haunting · Residual haunting · Electronic voice phenomenon · Spirit photography · Ectoplasm · Shadow people · Will-o'-the-wisp · Spirit possession · Demonic possession · Demon · Demonology · Exorcism · Paranormal television · Paranormal fiction · Afterlife · Reincarnation · Spirit world · Spiritualism · Ouija · Conjuration · Clairvoyance · Mediumship · Psychic · Psychic reading · Remote viewing · Extra-sensory perception · Precognition · Near-death experience · Psychometry · Psychokinesis · Hypnosis · Telepathy · Parapsychology · Close encounter · Ufology · UFO · UFO sightings · Paranormal and occult UFO hypotheses · Cryptozoology · Cryptid
Articles on skepticism
Scientific skepticism · Hoax · Pseudoskepticism · Debunking · Cold reading · Magical thinking · Challenges for paranormal evidence · Committee for Skeptical Inquiry · James Randi Educational Foundation
Related articles on science, psychology, and logic
Anomalistics · Scientific method · Falsifiability · Pseudoscience · Fringe science · Protoscience · Fallacy · Argument from ignorance · Agnosticism · Uncertainty
Related articles on Social change and Parapsychology

Countermovement · Social movement · Death and culture · Parapsychology

- Online literature [2] of the Theosophical Society
- Astral Projection [3] at the Skeptic's Dictionary

Astrology

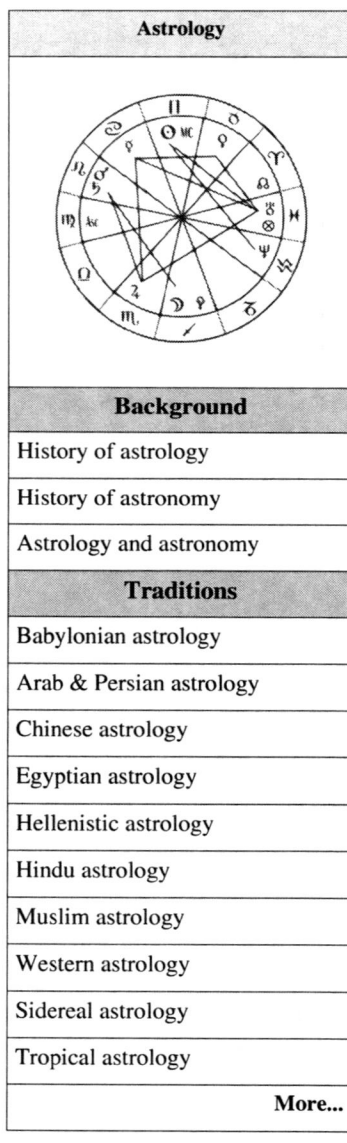

Astrology
Background
History of astrology
History of astronomy
Astrology and astronomy
Traditions
Babylonian astrology
Arab & Persian astrology
Chinese astrology
Egyptian astrology
Hellenistic astrology
Hindu astrology
Muslim astrology
Western astrology
Sidereal astrology
Tropical astrology
More...

Branches of horoscopic astrology
Natal astrology
Electional astrology
Horary astrology
Mundane astrology
More...
Categories
Astrologers
Astrological texts
Astrological writers
Astrology Portal

Part of a series of articles on the paranormal
Main articles
Paranormal · Supernatural · Occult · Forteana · Miracle · Magic · Aura · Ghost · Ghost hunting · Ghost story · Fear of ghosts · Poltergeist · Cold spot · Haunted locations: World, United States, United Kingdom · Haunted house · Intelligent haunting · Residual haunting · Electronic voice phenomenon · Spirit photography · Ectoplasm · Shadow people · Will-o'-the-wisp · Spirit possession · Demonic possession · Demon · Demonology · Exorcism · Paranormal television · Paranormal fiction · Afterlife · Reincarnation · Spirit world · Spiritualism · Ouija · Conjuration · Clairvoyance · Mediumship · Psychic · Psychic reading · Remote viewing · Extra-sensory perception · Precognition · Near-death experience · Psychometry · Psychokinesis · Hypnosis · Telepathy · Parapsychology · Close encounter · Ufology · UFO · UFO sightings · Paranormal and occult UFO hypotheses · Cryptozoology · Cryptid
Articles on skepticism
Scientific skepticism · Hoax · Pseudoskepticism · Debunking · Cold reading · Magical thinking · Challenges for paranormal evidence · Committee for Skeptical Inquiry · James Randi Educational Foundation
Related articles on science, psychology, and logic
Anomalistics · Scientific method · Falsifiability · Pseudoscience · Fringe science · Protoscience · Fallacy · Argument from ignorance · Agnosticism · Uncertainty
Related articles on Social change and Parapsychology
Countermovement · Social movement · Death and culture · Parapsychology

Astrology is a group of systems, traditions, and beliefs which hold that the relative positions of celestial bodies and related details can provide information about personality, human affairs and other "earthly" matters. A practitioner of astrology is called an astrologer. Few astrologers believe that the movements and positions of celestial bodies either directly influence life on Earth or correspond to events experienced on a human scale. More common is the idea that astrology is a symbolic language, an art form, or a form of divination. Despite differences in definitions, a common assumption of astrologers is that celestial placements can aid in the interpretation of past and present events, and in the prediction of the future.

Astrology is considered a pseudoscience or superstition by the scientific community, which sees a lack of statistically significant astrological predictions, while psychology explains much of the continued faith in astrology as a matter of cognitive biases. In 2006 the U.S. National Science Board published a statement which said it considers belief in ten survey items, astrology among them, to be "pseudoscientific".

Numerous traditions and applications employing astrological concepts have arisen since its earliest recorded beginnings in the 3rd millennium BC. Astrology has played an important role in the shaping of culture, early astronomy, the Vedas, and various disciplines throughout history. In fact, astrology and astronomy were often regarded as synonyms before the modern era, with the desire for predictive and divinatory knowledge one of the motivating factors for astronomical observation. Astronomy began to diverge from astrology after a period of gradual separation from the Renaissance up until the 18th century. Eventually, astronomy distinguished itself as the empirical study of astronomical objects and phenomena, without regard to the terrestrial implications of astrology.

The word "astrology" comes from the Latin term *astrologia* ("astronomy"), which in turn derives from the Greek noun αστρολογία: ἄστρον, *astron* ("constellation" or "star") and -λογία, *-logia* ("the study of"). The word "starcraft" has also traditionally been used to mean *astrology*.

Core beliefs

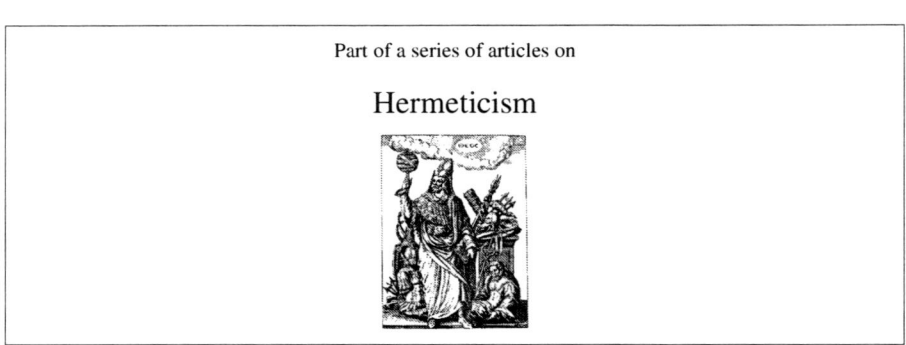

Part of a series of articles on

Hermeticism

Hermetic Religion
Hermeticism
Mythology
Hermes Trismegistus · Thoth · Poimandres
Hermetica
Corpus Hermeticum · Kybalion
Three Parts of the Wisdom of the Whole Universe
Alchemy · Astrology · Theurgy
Influence and Influences
Hermetic Movements
Rosicrucianism
Orders
Hermetic Order of the Golden Dawn · Hermetic Brotherhood of Luxor · Hermetic Brotherhood of Light
Topics in Hermetism
Qabalah Occult and divinatory tarot **Hermetists and Hermeticists** John Dee . Aleister Crowley · Israel Regardie Thābit ibn Qurra · Paracelsus Giordano Bruno · Samuel MacGregor Mathers · William Westcott Franz Bardon

The core beliefs of astrology were prevalent in parts of the ancient world and are epitomized in the Hermetic maxim, "as above, so below". Tycho Brahe used a similar phrase to summarize his studies in astrology: *suspiciendo despicio*, "by looking up I see downward". Although the principle that events in the heavens are mirrored by those on Earth was once generally held in most traditions of astrology around the world, in the West there has historically been a debate among astrologers over the nature of the mechanism behind astrology.

Although the connection between celestial mechanics and terrestrial dynamics was explored first by Isaac Newton with his development of a universal theory of gravitation, claims that the gravitational effects of the celestial bodies are what accounts for astrological generalizations are not substantiated by scientific research.

Most astrological traditions are based on the relative positions and movements of various real or construed celestial bodies and on the construction of implied or calculated celestial patterns as seen at the time and place of the event being studied. These are chiefly the astrological planets, the stars, the lunar nodes, Arabic parts and hypothetical planets. The frame of reference for such apparent positions is defined by the tropical or sidereal zodiac of twelve signs on one hand, and by the local horizon (ascendant-descendant axis) and midheaven-imum coeli axis on the other. This latter (local) frame is typically further divided into the twelve astrological houses. Furthermore, the astrological aspects are used to determine the geometric/angular relationship(s) between the various celestial bodies and angles in the horoscope.

Predictive astrology, in the Western tradition, employs two main methods: astrological transits and astrological progressions. In astrological transits the ongoing movements of the planets are interpreted for their significance as they transit through space and the horoscope. In astrological progressions the horoscope is progressed forward in time according to set methods. In Vedic astrology, the focus is on planetary periods to infer the trend, while transits are used to time significant events. Most Western astrologers no longer try to forecast actual events, but focus instead on general trends and developments. By comparison, Vedic astrologers predict both trends and events. Skeptics respond that this practice of western astrologers allows them to avoid making verifiable predictions, and gives them the ability to attach significance to arbitrary and unrelated events, in a way that suits their purpose.

In the past, astrologers often relied on close observation of celestial objects and the charting of their movements. Modern astrologers use data provided by astronomers which are transformed to a set of astrological tables called ephemerides, showing the changing zodiacal positions of the heavenly bodies through time.

Traditions

See also: List of astrological traditions, types, and systems

There are many traditions of astrology, some of which share similar features due to the transmission of astrological doctrines between cultures. Other traditions developed in isolation and hold different doctrines, though they too share some features due to drawing on similar astronomical sources.

Current traditions

The main traditions used by modern astrologers are Hindu Astrology (Jyotiṣa), Western astrology, and Chinese astrology.

Zodiac signs, 16th century European woodcut

Vedic and Western astrology share a common ancestry as horoscopic systems of astrology, in that both traditions focus on the casting of an astrological chart or horoscope, a representation of celestial entities, for an event based on the position of the Sun, Moon, and planets at the moment of the event. However, Vedic astrology uses the sidereal or fixed or constellational zodiac, linking the signs of the zodiac to their original constellations, while Western astrology uses the tropical or seasonal zodiac. Because of the precession of the equinoxes whose cycle is ~25,686 years long, during which the extensions of the polar axes describe circles, the twelve zodiacal signs in Western astrology no longer

correspond to the same part of the sky as their original constellations, due to centuries of change. In effect, in Western astrology the link between sign and constellation was broken in approximately 222

AD, whereas in Vedic astrology the constellations remain of paramount importance. Other differences between the two traditions include the use of 27 (or 28) nakshatras or lunar mansions, each 13⅓ degrees wide, which have been used in India since Vedic times, and the systems of planetary periods known as dashas.

In Chinese astrology, a quite different tradition has evolved. By contrast to Western and Indian astrology, the twelve signs of the zodiac do not divide the sky, but rather the celestial equator. The Chinese evolved a system in which each sign corresponds to one of twelve "double-hours" that govern the day, and to one of the twelve months. Each sign of the zodiac governs a different year, and combines with a system based on the five elements of Chinese cosmology to give a 60 (12 × 5) year cycle. The term *Chinese astrology* is used here for convenience, but it must be noted that versions of the same tradition exist in Korea, Japan, Vietnam, Thailand and other Asian countries. It appears that this is a remnant of a more ancient system of Jupiterian astrology, an astrological system primarily based on the motion of Jupiter, which orbits the Sun every 11.89 years.

Western astrology has been the result of the knowledge of the earlier Indian/Vedic and Egyptian schools (each developed in their own right, and neither shows traces of the later Babylonian influences) being diluted and simplified in passing first through Persia/Babylon, and then through Greece, and later Europe. In modern times, these traditions have come into closer contact with each other, notably with Indian and Chinese astrology having spread in more direct form to the West, while awareness of the modern notions of Western astrology is still fairly limited in Asia, and is not considered useful. Astrology in the Western world has diversified among some in modern times. New movements have appeared that have jettisoned much of more recent traditional astrology to concentrate on different approaches, such as a greater emphasis on midpoints, or a more psychological approach. Some recent Western developments include modern tropical and sidereal horoscopic astrology, including constellational and star or point-based astrology (including aspects to the fundamental planetary dynamics, such as perihelions and aphelions, and nodal points resulting from the inclinations of the planets' revolutionary planes to the Earth's ecliptic plane); heliocentric astrology, cosmobiology; psychological astrology; sun sign astrology; the Hamburg School of Astrology; and Uranian astrology, a subset of the Hamburg School.

Historical traditions

Throughout its long history, astrology has come to prominence in many regions and undergone developments and change. There are many astrological traditions that are historically important, but which have largely fallen out of use. Astrologers still retain an interest in them and regard them as an important resource. Historically significant traditions of astrology include Arab and Persian astrology (Medieval, Near East); Babylonian astrology (Ancient, Near East); Egyptian astrology; Hellenistic astrology (Classical antiquity); Hindu astrology and Mayan astrology.

Esoteric traditions

Many mystic or esoteric traditions have links to astrology. In some cases, such as Kabbalah, this involves participants incorporating elements of astrology into their own traditions. In other cases, many astrologers have incorporated other traditions into their own practice of astrology, and astrology has been incorporated into those traditions. Esoteric traditions include, but are not limited to, alchemy, chiromancy, Kabbalistic astrology, medical astrology, numerology, Rosicrucian or "Rose Cross", and Tarot divination.

Historically, alchemy in the Western World was particularly allied and intertwined with traditional Babylonian-Greek style astrology; in numerous ways they were built to complement each other in the search for occult or hidden knowledge. Astrology has used the concept of the four classical elements of alchemy from antiquity up until the present day. Traditionally, each of the seven planets in the solar system known to the ancients was associated with, held dominion over, and "ruled" a certain metal.

Horoscopic astrology

Main article: Horoscopic astrology

Horoscopic astrology is a system that some claim to have developed in the Mediterranean region and specifically Hellenistic Egypt around the late 2nd or early 1st century BC. However, horoscopic astrology has been practiced in India since ancient times, and Vedic astrology is the oldest surviving form of horoscopic astrology in the world. The tradition deals with two-dimensional diagrams of the heavens, or horoscopes, created for specific moments in time. The diagram is then used to interpret the inherent meaning underlying the alignment of celestial bodies at that moment based on a specific set of rules and guidelines. A horoscope was calculated normally for the moment of an individual's birth, or at the beginning of an enterprise or event, because the alignments of the heavens at that moment were thought to determine the nature of the subject in question. One of the defining characteristics of this form of astrology that makes it distinct from other traditions is the computation of the degree of the Eastern horizon rising against the backdrop of the ecliptic at the specific moment under examination, otherwise known as the ascendant. Horoscopic astrology is the most influential and widespread form of astrology in Africa, India, Europe and the Middle East. Medieval and most modern Western traditions of astrology have Hellenistic origins.

Horoscope

Central to horoscopic astrology and its branches is the calculation of the horoscope or astrological chart. This two-dimensional diagrammatic representation shows the celestial bodies' apparent positions in the heavens from the vantage of a location on Earth at a given time and place. The horoscope is also divided into twelve different celestial houses which govern different areas of life. Calculations performed in casting a horoscope involve arithmetic and simple geometry which serve to locate the apparent position of heavenly bodies on desired dates and times based on astronomical tables. In ancient Hellenistic astrology the ascendant demarcated the first celestial house of a horoscope. The word for the ascendant in Greek was ὡροσκόπος (*hōroskopos*) from which *horoscope* derives. In modern times, the word has come to refer to the astrological chart as a whole.

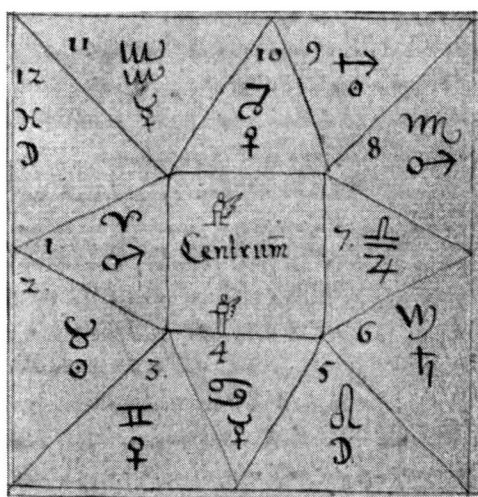

18th century Icelandic manuscript showing astrological houses and glyphs for planets and signs.

Branches

Traditions of horoscopic astrology can be divided into four branches that are each directed towards specific subjects or purposes. Often these branches use a unique set of techniques, or a different application of the core principles of the system to a different area. Many other subsets and applications of astrology are derived from these four fundamental branches.

Natal astrology is the study of a person's natal chart to gain information about the individual and their life experience. Katarchic astrology includes both electional and event astrology. The former uses astrology to determine the most auspicious moment to begin an enterprise or undertaking, and the latter to understand everything about an event from the time at which it took place. Horary astrology is used to answer a specific question by studying the chart of the moment the question is posed to an astrologer. Mundane or world astrology is the application of astrology to world events, including weather, earthquakes, and the rise and fall of empires or religions. This includes the Astrological Ages, such as the Age of Aquarius, Age of Pisces, and so on. Each age is about 2,150 years in length, and many people use these massive ages to characterize and describe major historical ages, as well as current developments in the world.

History

Main article: History of astrology

Many believe that the origins of much of the astrological doctrine and method that would later develop in Asia, Europe, and the Middle East are found among the ancient Babylonians and their system of celestial omens that began to be compiled around the middle of the 2nd millennium BC. They believe this system of celestial omens later spread, either directly or indirectly through the Babylonians and Assyrians, to other areas such as the Middle East, and Greece, where it merged with pre-existing indigenous forms of astrology. Thus, Babylonian astrology migrated to Greece, initially as early as the middle of the 4th century BC, and then around the late 2nd or early 1st century BC, after the Alexandrian conquests, this Babylonian astrology was mixed with the Egyptian tradition of decanic astrology to create horoscopic astrology. This new form of astrology, which appears to have originated in Alexandrian Egypt, spread across the ancient world into Europe, the Middle East, and India with varying degrees of influence.

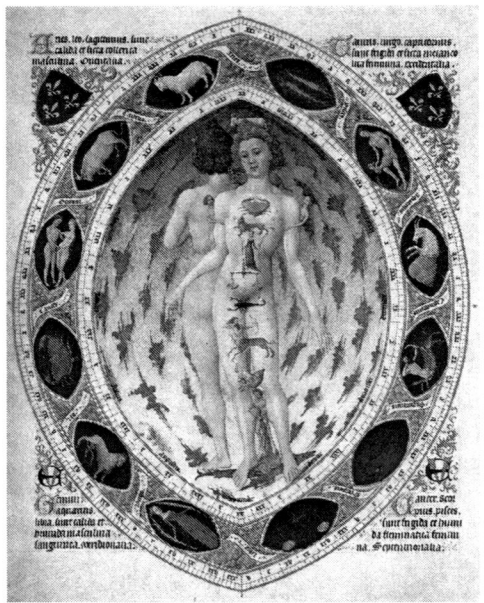

15th century image from the *Très Riches Heures du Duc de Berry* showing projected correlations between areas of the body and the zodiacal signs.

Before the modern era

The differentiation between astronomy and astrology varied from place to place; they were strongly linked in ancient India, ancient Babylonia and medieval Europe, but separated to an extent in the Hellenistic world. The first semantic distinction between astrology and astronomy was probably given by Isidore of Seville (see astrology and astronomy).

The pattern of astronomical knowledge gained from astrological endeavors has been historically repeated across numerous cultures, from ancient India through the classical Maya civilization to medieval Europe. Given this historical contribution, astrology has been called a protoscience along with disciplines such as alchemy.

Hand-colored version of the anonymous Flammarion woodcut (1888).

Astrology was not without criticism before the modern era; it was often challenged by Hellenistic skeptics, church authorities, and medieval Muslim astronomers, such as Al-Farabi (Alpharabius), Ibn al-Haytham (Alhazen), Abū Rayhān al-Bīrūnī, Avicenna and Averroes. Their reasons for refuting astrology were often due to both scientific (the methods used by astrologers being conjectural rather than empirical) and religious (conflicts with orthodox Islamic scholars) reasons. Ibn Qayyim Al-Jawziyya (1292–1350), in his *Miftah Dar al-SaCadah*, used empirical arguments in astronomy in order to refute astrology and divination.

Many prominent thinkers, philosophers and scientists, such as Galen, Paracelsus, Girolamo Cardan, Nicolaus Copernicus, Taqi al-Din, Tycho Brahe, Galileo Galilei, Johannes Kepler, Carl Jung and others, practiced or significantly contributed to astrology.

Contemporary changes

Several innovations have occurred in contemporary astrological practice.

Western

Main article: Western astrology

During the middle of the 20th century, Alfred Witte and, following him, Reinhold Ebertin pioneered the use of midpoints (see Midpoint (astrology)) in horoscopic analysis. From the 1930s to the 1980s, astrologers including Dane Rudhyar, Liz Greene and Stephen Arroyo pioneered the use of astrology for psychological analysis, with some following the lead of psychologists like Carl Jung. In the 1930s, Don Neroman developed and popularized in Europe a form of Locational Astrology under the name of

"Astrogeography". In the 1970s, American astrologer Jim Lewis developed and popularized a different approach under the name of Astrocartography. Both methods purport to identify varying life conditions through differences in location.

Vedic (Hindu astrology)

Main article: Vedic astrology

Indian astrology uses a different zodiac than Western astrology and is a branch of Vedic science. In India, there is a long-established widespread belief in astrology, and it is commonly used for daily life, foremost with regard to marriages, and secondarily with regard to career and electional and karmic astrology. In the 1960s, H.R. Seshadri Iyer, introduced a system including the concepts of yogi and avayogi. It generated interest with research oriented astrologers in the West. From the early 1990s, Indian vedic astrologer and author, V.K. Choudhry has created and developed the Systems' Approach for Interpreting Horoscopes, a simplified system of Jyotish (predictive astrology) The system, also known as "SA", helps those who are trying to learn Jyotisha. The late K.S. Krishnamurti developed the Krishnamurti Paddhati system based on the analysis of the stars (nakshatras), by sub-dividing the stars in the ratio of the dasha of the concerned planets. The system is also known as "KP" and "sub theory". In 2001, Indian scientists and politicians debated and critiqued a proposal to use state money to fund research into Vedic astrology.

Effects on world culture

Main article: Cultural influence of astrology

Belief in astrology holds firm today in many parts of the world: in one poll, 31% of Americans expressed a belief in astrology and, according to another study, 39% considered it scientific.

Astrology has had an influence on both language and literature. For example, influenza, from medieval Latin *influentia* meaning influence, was so named because doctors once believed epidemics to be caused by unfavorable planetary and stellar influences. The word "disaster" comes from the Italian *disastro*, derived from the negative prefix *dis-* and from Latin *aster* "star", thus meaning "ill-starred". Adjectives "lunatic" (Luna/Moon), "mercurial" (Mercury), "venereal" (Venus), "martial" (Mars), "jovial" (Jupiter/Jove), and "saturnine" (Saturn) are all old words used to describe personal qualities said to resemble or be highly influenced by the astrological characteristics of the planet, some of which are derived from the attributes of the ancient Roman gods they are named after. In literature, many writers, notably Geoffrey Chaucer and William Shakespeare, used astrological symbolism to add subtlety and nuance to the description of their characters' motivation(s). More recently, Michael Ward has proposed that C.S. Lewis imbued his *Chronicles of Narnia* with the characteristics and symbols of the seven heavens. Often, an understanding of astrological symbolism is needed to fully appreciate such literature.

Some modern thinkers, notably Carl Jung, believe in astrology's descriptive powers regarding the mind without necessarily subscribing to its predictive claims. In education astrology is reflected in the university education of medieval Europe, which was divided into seven distinct areas, each represented by a particular planet and known as the seven liberal arts. Dante Alighieri speculated that these arts, which grew into the sciences we know today, fitted the same structure as the planets. In music the best known example of astrology's influence is in the orchestral suite called "The Planets" by the British composer Gustav Holst, the framework of which is based upon the astrological symbolism of the planets.

Astrology and science

Pseudoscientific concepts
Claims
Measurable correlations can be reliably found between the position of the planets and personality and human events.
Related scientific disciplines
Astronomy, Psychology
Year proposed
antiquity
Original proponents
ancient priests and astrologers
Subsequent proponents
Philip Berg, Michel Gauquelin, Linda Goodman, Liz Greene, Alan Leo, Sydney Omarr, Joan Quigley, Jackie Stallone, Athena Starwoman, Shelley von Strunckel, Richard Tarnas

In the Islamic world astrology was rejected during the turn of the 2nd millennium AD owing to the development of the scientific method and the work of al-Farabi, Alhacen, al-Biruni, Avicenna and Averroes, who made a semantic distinction between astronomy and astrology and helped to render astrology obsolete for Muslims. Muslim views on astrology have generally remained negative.

By the time of Francis Bacon and the scientific revolution, newly emerging scientific disciplines acquired a method of systematic empirical induction based upon experimental observations. At this point, astrology and astronomy began to diverge; astronomy became regarded as one of the empirical sciences, while astrology came to be understood as a part of scholastic metaphysics, and was increasingly viewed as an occult science or superstition by natural scientists. For example, Christiaan Huygens wrote in his *Cosmotheoros*: "And as for the Judicial Astrology, that pretends to foretel what is to come, it is such a ridiculous, and oftentimes mischievous Folly, that I do not think it fit to be so much as named." This separation accelerated through the 18th and 19th centuries.

Contemporary scientists, such as Richard Dawkins and Stephen Hawking, regard astrology as unscientific, and those such as Andrew Fraknoi of the Astronomical Society of the Pacific have labeled it a pseudoscience. In 1975, the American Humanist Association characterized those who have faith in astrology as doing so "in spite of the fact that there is no verified scientific basis for their beliefs, and indeed that there is strong evidence to the contrary". Astronomer Carl Sagan was unwilling to sign the statement, not because he felt astrology was valid, but because he found the statement's tone authoritarian. Sagan stated that he would instead have been willing to sign a statement describing and refuting the principal tenets of astrological belief, which he believed would have been more persuasive and would have produced less controversy than the circulated statement.

Astrophysicist Neil deGrasse Tyson asserted that "astrology was discredited 600 years ago with the birth of modern science. 'To teach it as though you are contributing to the fundamental knowledge of an informed electorate is astonishing in this, the 21st century'. Education should be about knowing how to think, 'And part of knowing how to think is knowing how the laws of nature shape the world around us. Without that knowledge, without that capacity to think, you can easily become a victim of people who seek to take advantage of you'".

Although astrology has not been considered a science for some time, it has been the subject of considerable research by astrologers since the beginning of the 20th century. In their study of 20th-century research into natal astrology, Geoffrey Dean, a former astrologer who became critical of the field, and coauthors documented this burgeoning research activity performed primarily within the astrological community.

Research

Studies have repeatedly failed to demonstrate statistically significant relationships between astrological predictions and operationally defined outcomes. Effect size tests of astrology-based hypotheses conclude that the mean accuracy of astrological predictions is no greater than what is expected by chance. For example, when testing for cognitive, behavioral, physical and other variables, one study of 2000 astrological "time twins" born within minutes of each other did not show a celestial influence on human characteristics. It has been suggested that other statistical research is often wrongly seen as evidence for astrology due to uncontrolled artifacts.

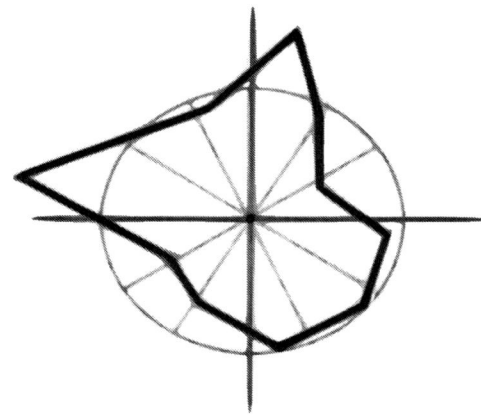

The Mars effect: relative frequency of the diurnal position of Mars in the birth chart of "eminent athletes"Wikipedia:Please clarify (after Michel Gauquelin 1991Wikipedia:Citing sources).

Experimental psychologists have suggested that several different psychological phenomena can contribute to perception of astrological accuracy. One, related to confirmation bias, is that people who are given a set of multiple predictions tend to remember more of the accurate predictions ("hits") than the inaccurate ones ("misses"). Consequently, people tend to recall the set of predictions as being more accurate than it actually was. When astrological predictions turn out to correspond with some phenomena but not with others, the recollected integrity of these predictions may stem in part from this phenomenon. A second, called the Forer effect, is that individuals tend to give high accuracy ratings to descriptions of their personality that are presented to them as tailored specifically for them, but which are in fact vague and general enough to apply to a wide range of people. When predictions use vague language, the appearance that they are specific to the individual may be partially attributable to the Forer effect.

The French psychologist and statistician who devoted his life to the attempt to demonstrate the validity of certain fundamentals of astrology, Michel Gauquelin, wrote that he had found correlations between some planetary positions and certain human traits such as vocations. Gauquelin's most widely known concept is the Mars effect, which denotes a correlation between the planet Mars occupying certain positions in the sky more often at the birth of eminent sports champions than at the birth of ordinary people. A similar idea is explored by Richard Tarnas in his work *Cosmos and Psyche*, in which he examines correspondences between planetary alignments and historically significant events and individuals. Since its original publication in 1955, the Mars effect has been the subject of critical studies and skeptical publications which aim to refute it, and of studies in fringe journals used to support or expand the original ideas. Gauquelin's research has not received mainstream scientific notice.

Obstacles to research

Astrologers have argued that there are significant obstacles in carrying out scientific research into astrology today, including lack of funding, lack of background in science and statistics by astrologers, and insufficient expertise in astrology by research scientists and skeptics. Some astrologers have argued that few practitioners today pursue scientific testing of astrology because they feel that working with clients on a daily basis provides personal validation for their clients.

Another argument made by astrologers is that most studies of astrology do not reflect the nature of astrological practice and that the scientific method does not apply to astrology. Some astrology proponents argue that the prevailing attitudes and motives of many opponents of astrology introduce conscious or unconscious bias in the formulation of hypotheses to be tested, the conduct of the tests, and the reporting of results.

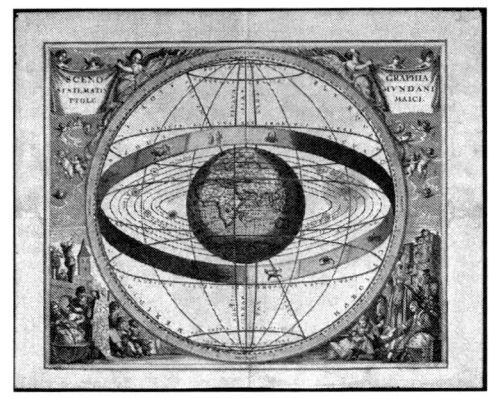

The Ptolemaic system depicted by Andreas Cellarius, 1660/61

Mechanism

Astrologers have not presented consistent explanations of physical mechanisms underlying astrological beliefs, and few modern astrologers believe in a direct causal relationship between heavenly bodies and earthly events. An editorial published by the Astronomical Society of the Pacific reports no evidence for a scientifically defined mechanism by which celestial objects can influence terrestrial affairs. Researchers have posited acausal, purely correlative, relationships between astrological observations and events, such as the theory of synchronicity proposed by Carl Jung. Others have posited a basis in divination. Others have argued that empirical correlations stand on their own epistemologically, and do not need the support of any theory or mechanism. To some observers, and most astrologers, these non-mechanistic concepts raise serious questions about the feasibility of validating astrology through scientific testing, and some have gone so far as to reject the applicability of the scientific method to astrology entirely. Some astrologers, a minority, on the other hand, believe that astrology is amenable to the scientific method, given sufficiently sophisticated analytical methods, and they cite pilot studies to support this view. Consequently, several astrologers have called for or advocated continuing studies of astrology based on statistical validation.

Early geometry was connected to the divine for most medieval scholars. The compass in this 13th century manuscript is a symbol of God's act of creation via the divine or perfect circle.

See also

- Astrological organizations
- Astrological symbols
- Astrology and astronomy
- Astrology and computers
- Astrological age
- Age of Aquarius
- Credulity
- Da Liu Ren

- List of astrologers
- List of astrological traditions, types, and systems
- Planets in astrology
- Pseudoscience
- Qi Men Dun Jia
- Season of birth
- Superstition
- www.nakshatralok.com [1]

Further reading

- Jay Agarwal, *East Meets West: Fun, Accurate and Honest Personality Insights* (Combines Western astrology with Chinese astrology), Analisa Enterprises, LLC, 2008. ISBN 978-0-9798572-0-1
- Roger Beck, A Brief History of Ancient Astrology, Blackwell (2007)
- Nicholas Campion, *A History of Western Astrology* Vol. 1, The Ancient World, Continuum, 2009. ISBN 978-1-84725-214-2 (first published as *The Dawn of Astrology: a Cultural History of Western Astrology Volume 1*, Continuum,2008).
- Nicholas Campion, *A History of Western Astrology* Vol. 2, The Medieval and Modern Worlds, Continuum 2009. ISBN 978-1-84725-224-1.

External links

- Astrology [2] at the Open Directory Project
- Astronomical Pseudo-Science: A Skeptic's Resource List [3] from the Astronomical Society of the Pacific

Automatic writing

Part of a series on
Spiritualism
Spirit · Spiritualism
Spiritualist beliefs
Spiritism
Practices
Mediumship · Obsession
Spirit possession
Séance · Fortune-telling
Faith healing ·
Psychometry
Automatic writing · Ouija
Organizations
Spiritualist Church
National Union
Related topics
Afterlife
Spirit world · Spirit guide
Shamanism · Animism
Psychic · Clairvoyant
Paranormal · Occult
Parapsychology

Automatic writing is the alleged process or production of writing material that proponents claim does not come from the conscious thoughts of the writer. Practitioners say that the writer's hand forms the message, with the person being unaware of what will be written. In some cases, it is done by people in an alleged trance state. In others, the writer is aware (not in a trance) of their surroundings but claims not to be aware of the actions of their writing hand.

History

George (Georgie) Hyde-Lees, the wife of William Butler Yeats, said that she could write automatically. In 1975, Wendy Hart of Maidenhead said that she wrote automatically about Nicholas Moore, a sea captain who died in 1642. Her husband did research on Moore, and he said that this person had resided at St Columb Major in Cornwall during the Civil War.

Spiritual Automatic Writing

Main article: Spiritism

Automatic writing, or psychography, is a concept in spiritism by which spirits are claimed to dictate or take the hand of a medium to write messages, letters, and even entire books.

Criticism

A 1998 article in *Psychological Science* described a series of experiments designed to determine whether people who believed in automatic writing could be shown that it might be the ideomotor effect. The paper indicated that "our attempt to introduce doubt about the validity of automatic writing did not succeed." The paper noted that "including information about the controversy surrounding facilitated communication did not affect self-efficacy ratings, nor did it affect the number of responses that were produced. In this sense, illusory facilitation appears to be a very robust phenomenon, not unlike illusory correlation, which is not reversed by warning participants about the phenomenon."

Psychology professor Théodore Flournoy investigated the claim by 19th-century medium Hélène Smith (Catherine Müller) that she did automatic writing to convey messages from Mars in Martian language. Flournoy concluded that her "Martian" language had a strong resemblance to Ms. Smith's native language of French. Flournoy concluded that her automatic writing was "romances of the subliminal imagination, derived largely from forgotten sources (for example, books read as a child)." He invented the term cryptomnesia to describe this phenomenon.

Further reading

- Carroll, Robert Todd. "Automatic writing" [1]. *The Skeptic's Dictionary*. 2003. ISBN 0-471-27242-6.
- Randi, James. "Automatic writing" [2]. *An Encyclopedia of Claims, Frauds, and Hoaxes of the Occult and Supernatural*. 1995. ISBN 0-312-15119-5.

See also

- Artistic inspiration
- Asemic writing
- Automatic speech
- Hypergraphia
- Matthew Manning
- Ouija

B

Banishing

In Ceremonial magic, **banishing** refers to one or more rituals intended to remove non-physical influences ranging from spirits to negative influences. It is often used as a component of a more complex ceremony, although it can be performed by itself as well. Banishing can be viewed as one of several techniques of magick, closely related to ritual purification and a typical prerequisite for consecration and invocation.

For "actual working" Crowley recommends a short, general banishing, with a comment that "In more elaborate ceremonies it is usual to banish everything by name."

The rituals

In the Hermetic Order of the Golden Dawn, the Lesser Banishing Ritual of the Pentagram (LBRP for shorthand) must be learned by the Neophyte before moving on to the next grade (Zelator).

Other Golden Dawn banishing rituals include the *Greater Banishing Ritual of the Pentagram*, and the banishing rituals of the hexagram.

See also

- Ritual
- Exorcism

Bibliomancy

Bibliomancy is the use of books in divination. The method of employing sacred books (especially specific words and verses) for 'magical medicine', for removing negative entities, or for divination is widespread in many religions of the world:

> *What the Vedas were to the Hindus, Homer to the Greeks, and Ovid and Virgil to the Romans, the Old Testament was to the Jews, the Old and New Testaments to the Christians, and the Koran and Hafiz to the Mohammedans.* -- Jewish Encyclopedia, 1906 edition

Terminology

According to the *Oxford English Dictionary*, the word **bibliomancy** (etymologically from *biblio-* "books" and *-mancy* "divination by means of") "divination by books, or by verses of the Bible" was first recorded in 1753 (*Chambers' Cyclopedia*). Sometimes this term is used synonymously with **stichomancy** (from *sticho-* "row, line, verse") "divination by lines of verse in books taken at hazard", which was first recorded ca. 1693 (Urquhart's *Rabelais*).

Bibliomancy compares with *rhapsodomancy* (from *rhapsode* "poem, song, ode") "divination by reading a random passage from a poem". A historical precedent was the ancient Roman practice of sortes "sortilege, divination by drawing lots", which specialized into *sortes Homerica*, *sortes Virgilianae*, and *sortes Sanctorum*, using the texts of Homer, Virgil, and the Bible.

History

Although some Christian and Jewish groups believe that it forbids divination in general, Leviticus strictly forbids *nahash* and *onan*. The literal meaning of *nahash* is *hissing*, though it can be extended to *whispering*, and it has historically been understood to refer to enchantment; *onan* literally translates as *clouds*, possibly referring to nephomancy.

According to the Shulchan Aruch (Rema, Yoreh Deah, 179), it is not a committal of the sin of necromancy to divine an answer using the "goral", being the practice of opening the Chumash to see an answer to a question, or asking a child for the first piece of scripture that comes to his mind.

Method

1. A book is picked that is believed to hold truth.
2. It is balanced on its spine and allowed to fall open.
3. A passage is picked, with the eyes closed.

Among Christians, the Bible is most commonly used (in the *Sortes Sanctorum*), and in Islamic cultures the Qur'an. In the Middle Ages the use of Virgil's *Aeneid* was common in Europe and known as the *sortes Virgilianae*. In the classical world the *sortes Virgilianae* and *sortes Homerica* (using the *Iliad* and *Odyssey*) were used.

In Iran , Bibliomancy using the dīvān of Hafez is the most popular for this kind of divination, but by no means the only kind. The Qur'an, as well as the Masnawī of Rumi may also be used. Fāl-e Ḥafez may be used for one or more persons. In group bibliomancy, the dīvān will be opened at random, and beginning with the ode of the page that one chances upon, each ode will be read in the name of one of the individuals in the group. The ode is the individual's fāl. Assigning of the odes to individuals depends on the order in which the individuals are seated and is never random. One or three verses from the ode following each person's fāl is called the šāhed, which is read after the recitation of the fāl. According to another tradition the šāhed is the first or the seventh verse from the ode following the fāl . An ode which had already been used for one individual in the group is disqualified from serving as the fāl for a second time .

Because book owners frequently have favorite passages that the books open themselves to, some practitioners use dice or another randomiser to choose the page to be opened. This practice was formalized by the use of coins or yarrow stalks in consulting the I Ching. Tarot divination can also be considered a form of bibliomancy, with the main difference that the cards (pages) are unbound.

There is a prevalent practice among certain, particularly messianic, members of Chabad-Lubavitch Chasidic movement to use the Igrot Kodesh, a thirty-volume collection of letters written by their leader Menachem Mendel Schneerson for guidance.

Another variant requires the selection of a random book from a library before selecting the random passage from that book. This also holds if a book has fallen down from a shelf on its own. English poet Robert Browning used this method to ask about the fate of his enchantment to Elizabeth Barret (later known as Elizabeth Barret Browning). He was at first disappointed to choose the book "Cerutti's Italian Grammar", but on randomly opening it his eyes fell on the following sentence: 'if we love in the other world as we do in this, I shall love thee to eternity' (which was a translation exercise).

Bibliomancy in fiction

In *Michael Strogoff* (1876) by Jules Verne, Feofar Khan judged Michael Strogoff to blindness after pointing randomly in the Koran at the phrase: "And he will no more see the things of this earth.".

In *The Book of Webster's* (1993) by J. N. Williamson, the sociopathic protagonist Dell uses the dictionary to guide his actions.

In 'The Ash Tree' by M.R. James, bibliomancy is used to produce a warning message from the bible.

The popular 'lonelygirl15' internet fiction series mentions the use of bibliomancy as part of the main character's religious beliefs.

The novel The First Verse by Barry McCrea tells the story of Niall Lenihan, a student who falls in with a 'cult' whose members use *sortes* to guide them.

In the novel *Man in the High Castle* by Philip K. Dick, every major character uses bibliomancy, mainly by casting yarrow stalks in conjunction with the I Ching. Dick himself reportedly used this process for deciding key points in the story, even going so far as to blaming the I Ching for plot developments that he himself did not particularly care for.

In Wilkie Collins' 1868 novel *The Moonstone*, the narrator Gabriel Betteredge routinely practices bibliomancy using the pages of Daniel Defoe's *Robinson Crusoe*.

In Lirael, by Garth Nix, *The Black Book of Bibliomancy*, a fake book, is mentioned.

Trivia

- Bibliomancy is a school of magic available in the horror roleplaying game Unknown Armies.

External links

- *Bibliomancy* from the Jewish Encyclopedia [1]
- Free Bibliomancy readings from multiple literary sources at bibliomancy.org [2]
- Free Online Stichomancy Readings at Facade.com [3]
- *Bibliomancy* from A Word A Day [4]

Biosophy

Biosophy, meaning *wisdom of life*, is a humanist movement heavily influenced by the 17th-century philosopher Baruch Spinoza. It is "the science and art of intelligent living based on the awareness and practice of spiritual values, ethical-social principles and character qualities essential to individual freedom and social harmony" [1]. It stands in contrast to biology, which can be broadly described as the *understanding of life*.

History

The term **Biosophy** was probably first used in 1806 by Ignaz Paul Vitalis Troxler, a Swiss philosopher whose early works followed F. W. J. Schelling. It was later used by other philosophers like Peter Wessel Zapffe (1899-1990), who used biology as the foundation of his philosophy. Zapffe first set out his ideas in Den sidste Messias (en. *The Last Messiah*) (1933). Later Zapffe gave a more systematic defence in his philosophical treatise *Om det tragiske* (en. *On the tragic*) (1941). The Biosophical Institute claims that Dr. Frederick Kettner (1886-1957) was the founder of biosophy [2]. Kettner was himself originally inspired by the organicism of Constantin Brunner.

Contemporary 'biosophers' include Jong Bhak, who defines Biosophy as a "new way of performing philosophy generated from scientific and biological awareness" [3]. Bhak developed his theory of Biosophy while studying at Cambridge university in 1995 and afterwards. The main difference of Bhak's biosophy from other philosophy is that his biosophy is a computable philosophy. It borrows Russell's logicism and extends it to a computational set of ideas and knowledge. One ultimate aim of biosophy is to construct a logical thinking machine that can do philosophy for human beings. See more on this [4].

Theory of Biosophy

Zapffe's arguments have been understood in relation to philosophical pessimism and existentialism. He is also sometimes regarded as a nihilist.

The Biosophy Program was presented on the Internet by Anna Öhman & Svenolov Lindgren in January 1998 [5]. They noted that "the term biosophy was previously used by Zapffe (1941) in a literary context for the analysis of human social life based on philosophy of existence and biological facts. Such a narrow circumscription of biosophy is in our opinion no obstacle to widen the definition to encompass all systematic thinking on biological issues."

The Biosophy Program was intended to circumscribe and systemize biological studies in a philosophical framework to support teaching at courses on philosophy and courses on biology. The biosophical thinking is defined by Öhman & Lindgren in five philosophical fields and discriminated from Næss' ecosophy.

Objectives

- To create biosophical groups for character and peace education where the individual has opportunities of self-improvement.
- To encourage integration among individuals based on their mutual interest in a spiritual purpose in life.
- To network with other groups and organizations interested in character and peace education working cooperatively with them.
- To replace the blind acceptance of theological beliefs, superstitions and dogmas with the cultivation of spiritual intelligence as the basis for the Religion of Freedom and Friendship.
- To create a world-fellowship of peace-loving human beings who have overcome religious, national, racial and social prejudices who can work creatively for the growth of democracy, spiritual personal growth and world peace.
- To work for the synthesis of religion, philosophy, science, education and art.
- To perpetuate and advance Dr. Frederick Kettner's principles and work for the development and cultivation of the character and peace nature in young people.
- To create a Peace Department in the national governments headed by a Secretary of Peace, and to establish peace universities.
- To establish a world-fellowship of thinking human beings who can work creatively for the growth of spiritual democracy and world peace.
- To cooperate in the advancement of humanity from civilization to the age of soulization.

See also

- Biology
- Bioinformatics
- Biophysics

External links

- Essay at Ecognosis [6]
- The Biosophical Institute [1]
- BioSophy.org [4]

Black magic

Black magic is the belief of practices of magic that draws on assumed malevolent powers. This type of magic is invoked when wishing to kill, steal, injure, cause misfortune or destruction, or for personal gain without regard to harmful consequences to others. As a term, "black magic" is normally used by those that do not approve of its uses, commonly in a ritualistic setting; the argument of "magic having no colour, and it is merely the application and use by its user," backs the claim that not everything termed as "black magic" has malevolent intentions behind it, and some would consider it to have beneficial and benevolent uses. These uses could include killing diseases or pests.

Practitioners who use magic in this way argue that the effect itself is malevolent by causing death to insects (as in the above example), but as an indirect consequence of black magic, good can be a result, such as in the form of less pests around. In this school of thought, there is no separation between benevolent and malevolent magic as there is no universal morality against which magic can be measured. A rather different view on Black Magic is used in the system of Chaos Magick. In this branch of occult practice, spells sometimes correspond to colours, depending on the supposed effect (i.e, red-magick, which is magic concerned with combat, such as low-level curses). Black Magic, according to Chaos Magick, corresponds to magic that is performed around the themes of death, separation, severance and entropy. This can refer to powerful curses meant to bring the strongest effect, spells to sever emotional ties to objects or people, and so on.

In fiction, black magic will quite frequently be synonymous with evil, such is the case in Rosemary's Baby, J.K. Rowling's Harry Potter series (referred to as *the dark arts* in the novels), and Shakespeare's Macbeth, with many other examples existing. In many popular video games, such as *Final Fantasy*, white and black magic is simply used to distinguish between healing/defensive spells (such as a "cure") and offensive/elemental spells (such as "fire") respectively, and does not carry an inherent good or evil connotation.

Black and white magic differences

The differences between what is considered black magic and white magic are debatable, though generally can fall within the following broad categories:

- The **All as One** theory states that all forms of magic are evil, irrespective of colour (white or black). This view is generally associated with Satanism. People that maintain this opinion include those belonging to most branches of Christianity and Islam.
- The **Dark Doctrine** theory states that black magic is the powers of darkness, usually seen from a Left-Hand Path point of view. This may or may not contrast with white magic, depending on the user's acceptance of dualism.

- The **Formal Differences** theory states that the forms and components of black magic are not the same due to the different aims or interests of those casting harmful spells than those of white. Harmful spell-casting tends to include symbolism that seems hazardous or harmful to human beings, such as sharp, pointed, prickly, caustic, and hot element(s) combined with very personal objects from the spell's target (their hair, blood, mementos, etc.). This distinction can primarily be observed in folk magic, but pertains to other types of magic also.
- The **No Connection** theory states that both black and white magic are completely different from the base up and are accomplished uniquely, even if they achieve similar effects. This stance is often presented in fiction, and as a result, the two classes of magic-users are portrayed as being both ideologically and diametrically opposed. In *The Lord of the Rings*, the Elves find it strange that Humans and Hobbits can even use a single word, "magic", which refers to both forms, as the Elvish tongues regard them also linguistically as completely separate and unrelated.
- The **Separate but Equal** theory states that black and white magic are exactly the same thing, differentiated only by their end goals and intent. According to this theory, the same spell could be either white or black *(see gray magic)*; its nature is determined by the end result of the spell. The majority of religions follow this belief, as does the remainder of fiction that does not follow the *No Connection* theory. By this interpretation, even such spells commonly seen as good can be misused, so healing could be used to regenerate the body to the point of cancer, for instance.

Black magic practices

Within common mainstream religion, such as Christianity and modern Paganism to an extent, there are certain taboos surrounding forms of magic. Although culture may place certain forms of magic in one side or another of this spectrum, there are in fact some cultural universals about free will,

- True name spells - the theory that knowing a person's true name allows control over that person, making this wrong for the same reason. This can also be used as a connection to the other person, or to free them from another's compulsion, so it is in the grey area,
- Immortalirituals - from a Taoist perspective, life is finite, and wishing to live beyond one's natural span is not with the flow of nature. Beyond this, there is a major issue with immortality. Because of the need to test the results, the subjects must be killed. Even a spell to extend life may not be entirely good, especially if it draws life energy from another to sustain the spell,
- Necromancy - for purposes of usage, this is defined not as general black magic, but as any magic having to do with death itself, either through divination of entrails, or the act of raising the dead bodily, as opposed to resurrection or CPR,
- Curses/Hexes - a curse can be as simple as wishing something bad would happen to another, to a complex ritual.

Black magic as part of religion

Many rituals performed by black magic practitioners mentioned on television are mentioned as having aspects similar to Christianity though in a perverted form, and it appears to be universally based upon a religion, but using perverted rituals to suit the needs of the user.[citation needed] For example, black magic users might invert a pentacle just as Satanists invert a cross. Likewise, corrupted rites or sacrifice may substitute blood or faeces for the water or wine. Seen from this perspective, the distinction between black and white magic would be simple,

- White magic would be the original rituals, which embody the tenets of the religion in question. For Buddhism or Hinduism, this might be long and complex prayer sutras. Taoist and Shinto magic would largely be based upon fertility and nature rituals, and
- Black magic would be a corruption or misuse of such above rituals, using them to self-serving or destructive ends without regard for the cultural morals of the religion. This could be something such as making poppets to cause harm.

See also

- Necromancy
- Nigromancy
- Maleficium (sorcery)
- Demonology
- Gray magic
- White magic
- Witchcraft
- Ya sang
- Seiðr

Subtle body

A **subtle body** is one of a series of psycho-spiritual constituents of living beings, according to various esoteric, occult, and mystical teachings. Each subtle body corresponds to a subtle plane of existence, in a hierarchy or great chain of being that culminates in the physical form.

It is known in different spiritual traditions; "the most sacred body" (*wujud al-aqdas*) and "supracelestial body" (*jism asli haqiqi*) in Sufism, "the diamond body" in Taoism and Vajrayana, "the light body" or "rainbow body" in Tibetan Buddhism, "the body of bliss" in Kriya Yoga, and "the immortal body" (*soma athanaton*) in Hermeticism. The various attributes of the subtle body are frequently described in terms of often obscure symbolism: Tantra features references to the sun and moon as well as various Indian rivers and deities, while Taoist alchemy speaks of cauldrons and cinnabar fields.

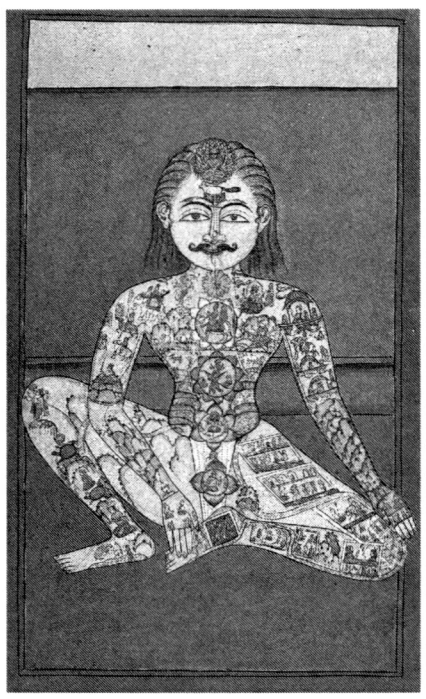

The subtle body in Indian mysticism, from a Yoga manuscript in Braj Bhasa language, 1899, now in the British Library.

Clairvoyants sometimes say that they can see the subtle bodies as an aura. The practice of astral projection, as described in various literature, is supposed to involve the separation of the subtle body from the physical. The theosophical movement was important in spreading such ideas throughout the West in the late 19th century. The existence of subtle bodies is unconfirmed by the mainstream scientific community.

Eastern Esotericism

Chart showing the circulation of Qi energy, Ming Dynasty

See also: Taoism

The Yogic, Tantric and other systems of India, the Buddhist psychology of Tibet, as well as Chinese (Taoist alchemy) and Japanese (Shingon) esoterism are examples of doctrines that describe a subtle physiology having a number of focal points (chakras, acupuncture points) connected by a series of channels (nadis, Acupuncture meridians) that convey life-force (prana, vayu, ch'i, ki, lung).

These invisible channels and points are understood to determine the characteristics of the visible physical form. By understanding and mastering the subtlest levels of reality one gains mastery over the physical realm. Through practice of various breathing and visualisation exercises one is able to manipulate and direct the flow of vital force, to achieve superhuman (e.g. in martial arts) or miraculous powers ("siddhis") and attain higher states of consciousness, immortality, or liberation.

Hinduism

See also:

- Vedanta (the five *Koshas*)
- Samkhya
- Tantra
- Kundalini

The subtle body (***Sukshma sarira*** or *Sukshma sharira*) in Vedantic philosophy is composed of five Kosas or "sheaths". The subtle body is the vehicle of consciousness with which one passes from life to life. The **Liṅga Śarīra** is the vehicle of consciousness in later Samkhya, Vedanta, and Yoga , and is propelled by past-life tendencies, or *bhavas*. Linga can be translated as "characteristic mark" or "impermanence" and the term Sarira as "form" or "mold". *Karana* or "instrument" is a synonymous term. In the Classical Samkhya system of Isvarakrsna (ca. 4th century CE), the *Liṅga* is the characteristic mark of the transmigrating entity. It consists of twenty-five tattvas from eternal consciousness down to the five organs of sense, five of activity (*buddindriya* or *jñānendriya*, and *karmendriya* respectively) and the five subtle elements that are the objects of sense (*tanmatras*) The *Samkhyakarika* says:

"The subtle body (linga), previously arisen, unconfined, constant, inclusive of the great one (mahat) etc, through the subtle elements, not having enjoyment, transmigrates, (because of) being endowed with bhavas ("conditions" or "dispositions")

As a picture (does) not (exist) without a support, or as a shadow (does) not (exist) without a post and so forth; so too the instrument (linga or karana) does not exist without that which is specific (i.e. a subtle body)."

The idea was adopted by Vedanta and Yoga philosophy, and from there, in the 19th century, the terminology was adopted by the Theosophy of Madame Blavatsky. Subtility-The State Of Being Subtile To Will

Western esotericism

Planes of existence Gross and subtle bodies
Theosophy
Neo-Theosophy
Rosicrucian
The 7 Worlds & the 7 Cosmic Planes The Seven-fold constitution of Man The Ten-fold constitution of Man
Thelema
Body of light | Thelemic mysticism
Surat Shabda Yoga
Cosmology
Sufism
Sufi cosmology
Hinduism
Talas/Lokas - Tattvas, Kosas, Upadhis
Buddhism
Buddhist cosmology
Kabbalah
Atziluth -> Beri'ah -> Yetzirah -> Assiah Sephirot

Fourth Way
Ray of Creation
The Laws
Three Centers and Five Centers
Castaneda
The Double Body
The Second Attention
The Third Attention
The Dream Attention
The Realm of Inorganic Beings

Theosophy

H. P. Blavatsky's Theosophical teaching represented the convergence of 19th century Western occultism, Eastern philosophy, religion, science, and mysticism. *The Secret Doctrine*, and *The Key to Theosophy* combined the Vedantic concept of five koshas with Western esoteric traditions, (particularly Neoplatonism). She refers to a number of subtle bodies or vehicles of consciousness:

- *Linga Sharira* - the Double or Astral body
- *Kama rupa* - the "Desire Form"
- *Manas* - the Mind, Lower and Higher
- *Buddhi* - the Consciousness, Spiritual Soul (the vehicle of the Spirit)

The Linga Sarira or *Linga Sharira*, which is part of the **lower quaternary** is the *eidolon* of the Greeks, separated from the physical plane by a *Laya center*. It is the invisible double of the human body elsewhere referred to as the etheric body, etheric double, doppelgänger or bioplasmic body and serves as a model or matrix of the physical body, which conforms to the shape, appearance and condition of this "double".

The linga sarira can be separated or projected a limited distance from the body. When separated from the body it can be wounded by sharp objects. When it returns to the physical frame, the wound will be reflected in the physical counterpart, a phenomenon called "repercussion." At death, it is discarded together with the physical body and eventually disintegrates or decomposes. The mayavi-rupa, in contrast is an illusory body. Apparitions of the dead are often projections of the mayavi-rupa.

Theosophy was further systematised in the writings of C.W. Leadbeater and Annie Besant, who established the Adyar School of Theosophy or neo-Theosophy. They described seven bodies, but they divided Blavatsky's higher and lower astral and Manas into two bodies each:

- Etheric body
- Astral or emotional body
- Mental body (concrete mind)
- Causal body (abstract mind)

Each "body" has its own aura and set of chakras, and corresponds to a particular plane of existence. C.W. Leadbeater considered the astral body equivalent to the kama principle of Blavatsky's septenary series. Annie Besant wrote that the Linga Sarira corresponds to the *Etheric Double*, contrary to earlier theosophical teachings. The Linga Sarira is considered the vehicle of prana.

Post Theosophists

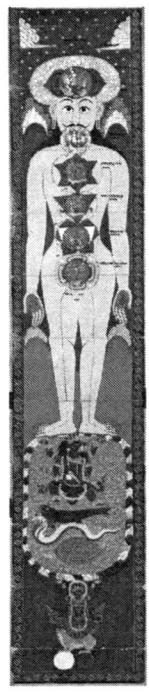

The Subtle body and the cosmic man, Nepal 1600's

The Adyar arrangement was taken up by Alice Bailey, and from there found its way (with variations) into the New Age worldview. It is also associated with the human aura observed through Kirlian photography and Kilner screens. The Anthroposophical view of the human being) found in Rudolf Steiner's Anthroposophical teachings usually referred to only the Etheric and Astral Bodies. However, Steiner also used a threefold classification of body, soul, and spirit as well as a sevenfold and a ninefold description.

Max Heindel divided the subtle body into: Vital Body made of Ether, our instrument for specializing the vital energy of the sun, seen by clairvoyant vision to extend about an inch and a half outside the body); the Desire body, which is our emotional nature and pervades both the vital and dense bodies, seen by clairvoyant vision to extend about 16 inches outside our visible body, related to the Desire World; and the Mental body, which functions like a mirror, reflects the outer world and enables the Ego to transmit its commands as thought, word and action. The human being is seen as a threefold Spirit, possessing a Mind by which he governs the threefold Body that he transmutes into a threefold Soul. The Human Spirit aspect has emanated from itself the desire body to be transmuted into the Emotional Soul; the Life Spirit aspect has emanated from itself the vital body to be transmuted into the Intellectual Soul; the Divine Spirit aspect has emanated from itself the dense body to be transmuted into the Conscious Soul.

Samael Aun Weor wrote extensively on the subtle vehicles, organizing them in accordance with the kabbalistic Tree of Life. The common person only contains the lunar vehicles of emotion (astral body), thought (mental body), and will (causal body), concentrations of the collective animalistic intelligence, the evolution of the Essence through the mineral, plant and animal kingdoms. Becoming human means to have a soul, a Solar Astral Body, Solar Mental Body and Solar Causal Body. These bodies are constructed through a form of Tantra called White tantrism.}}

Barbara Brennan's account of the subtle bodies in her books *Hands of Light* and *Light Emerging* refers to the subtle bodies as "layers" in the "Human Energy Field" or aura. Causality proceeds downwards: each of the layers has its own characteristics and can have its own expression of disease, requiring individual healing. As with the Adyar arrangement, each body or aura also has its own complement of chakras, which interrelate to those in the other layers.

Michal Levin describes the relationship between the energy bodies and the chakras in her book Meditation, Path to the Deepest Self.

Fourth Way

An interesting variant on the concept of subtle bodies is found in both Alchemical Taoism and the "Fourth Way" teachings of Gurdjieff and Ouspensky, where it is said that one can create a subtle body, and hence achieve post-mortem immortality, through spiritual or yogic exercises. The "soul" then is not something one is born with, but something that one has to develop through esoteric practice.

Aleister Crowley and the Body of Light

Thelema Category:Thelema

Core topics

The Book of the Law
Aleister Crowley
True Will · 93
Magick

Mysticism

Thelemic mysticism
The Great Work
Holy Guardian Angel
The Gnostic Mass

Thelemic texts

Works of Crowley
The Holy Books
Thelemite texts

Organizations

A∴A∴ · EGC · OTO
OSOGD · TO

Deities

Nuit · Hadit · Horus
Babalon · Chaos
Baphomet · Choronzon
Ankh-f-n-khonsu
Aiwass · Ma'at

Other topics

Stele of Revealing
Abrahadabra
Unicursal Hexagram
Abramelin oil
Thoth tarot deck

The work of the *Body of Light* was part of English author and occultist Aleister Crowley's system of magick, saying in his *Magick (Book 4)* that it must be developed by rigid discipline, including rituals and the "assumption of god-forms", as well as by practice and experience.

From Crowley's *Magick Without Tears* (Ch. 81):

> *One passes through the veil of the exterior world (which, as in Yoga, but in another sense, becomes "unreal" by comparison as one passes beyond) one creates a subtle body (instrument is a better term) called the body of Light; this one develops and controls; it gains new powers as one progresses, usually by means of what is called "initiation:" finally, one carries on almost one's whole life in this Body of Light, and achieves in its own way the mastery of the Universe.*

See also

Traditions

- Neoplatonism (the **okhemas**)
- Sufism
- Spiritism
- Hermeticism
- Theosophy (the Septenary, inspired by the five koshas of Vedanta)
- Anthroposophy (the etheric and astral bodies)
- Rosicrucianism, in the Western Wisdom Teachings philosophy (a *Seven-fold* and a *Ten-fold* constitution of Man)
- Thelemic mysticism
- Spiritual science

Other topics

- Aura
- Aureola
- biofield
- Clairvoyance
- Esoteric cosmology
- Kirlian photography
- Life review

- Reincarnation
- Perispirit
- Sex magic
- Silver cord
- Spiritual evolution
- Spirituality
- Mindstream
- Septenary (Theosophy)
- Tattwas

Further reading

- Alfass, Mirra (The Mother) *Mother's Agenda*
- Besant, Annie, *Man and His Bodies*
- Brennan, Barbara Ann, *Hands of Light : A Guide to Healing Through the Human Energy Field*, Bantam Books, 1987
- —, *Light Emerging: The Journey of Personal Healing*, Bantam Books, 1993
- Mircea Eliade, *Yoga: Immortality and Freedom*; transl. by W.R. Trask, Princeton University Press, 1969
- C. W. Leadbeater, *Man, Visible and Invisible*
- Sheila Ostrander and Lynn Schroeder *Psychic Discoveries Behind the Iron Curtain*, Englewood Cliffs, New Jersey: Prentice Hall, 1970.
- Poortman, J. J. *Vehicles of Consciousness; The Concept of Hylic Pluralism (Ochema)*, vol I-IV, The Theosophical Society in Netherlands, 1978
- Powell, Arthur E. *The Astral Body and other Astral Phenomena*
- —, *The Causal Body and the Ego*
- —, *The Etheric Double*
- —, *The Mental Body*
- Samael Aun Weor, *The Perfect Matrimony or The Door to Enter into Initiation*. Thelema Press. (1950) 2003.
- Samael Aun Weor, *The Esoteric Course of Alchemical Kabbalah* [1]. Thelema Press. (1969) 2007.
- Steiner, Rudolf, *Theosophy: An introduction to the supersensible knowledge of the world and the destination of man*. London: Rudolf Steiner Press. (1904) 1970
- —, *Occult science - An Outline*. Trans. George and Mary Adams. London: Rudolf Steiner Press, 1909, 1969
- Heindel, Max, *The Rosicrucian Mysteries (Chapter IV: The Constitution of Man: Vital Body - Desire Body - Mind* [2]), 1911, ISBN 0-911274-86-3
- Crowley, Aleister (1997). *Magick (Book 4)* 2nd ed. York Beach, Maine. : Samuel Weiser.

- Crowley, Aleister (1982). *Magick Without Tears.* Phoenix, AZ : Falcon Press
- Thelemapedia. (2004). *Body of Light* [3]. Retrieved April 16, 2006.
- White, John. Enlightenment and the Body of Light [4] in *What is Enlightenment?* magazine.
- James L. Oschman. Energy Medicine: The Scientific Basis.
- Levin, Michal. *Meditation, Path to the Deepest Self*, Dorling Kindersley, 2002. ISBN 978-0789483331
- Levin, Michal. *Spiritual Intelligence: Awakening the Power of Your Spirituality and Intuition.* Hodder & Stoughton, 2000. ISBN 978-0340733943

External links
- The Institute of Noetic Sciences [5] supporting research into supposed subtle body phenomena
- Astral Body in Theosophy and Neo-Theosophy (A comparison) [6]
- http://sped2work.tripod.com/sarira.html
- What are humans made of? http://www.spiritualresearchfoundation.org/articles/?id=spiritualresearch/spiritualscience/what-are-humans-comprised-of

C

Candomblé

Ilê Axé Iya Nassô Oká – Terreiro da Casa Branca

Afro-Brazilian topics
Afro-Brazilian history
Atlantic slave trade Slavery in Brazil Blanqueamiento List of Black Brazilians Kalunga Saros Racial democracy Pardo
Religion
Candomblé Umbanda Quimbanda
Culture
Capoeira

Candomblé (Portuguese pronunciation: [kẽdõˈblɛ]) is an African-originated or Afro-Brazilian religion, practised chiefly in Brazil by the "povo de santo" (people of saint). It originated in the cities of

Salvador, the capital of Bahia and Cachoeira, at the time one of the main commercial crossroads for the distribution of products and slave trade to other parts of Bahia state in Brazil. Although Candomblé is practiced primarily in Brazil, it is also practiced in other countries in the Americas, including Uruguay, Argentina, Venezuela, Colombia, Panama and Mexico, and in Europe in Germany, Italy, Portugal and Spain. The religion is based in the anima (soul) of Nature, and is also known as Animism. It was developed in Brazil with the knowledge of African Priests that were enslaved and brought to Brazil, together with their mythology, their culture and language, between 1549 and 1888.

The rituals involve the possession of the initiated by Orishas, offerings and sacrifices of the mineral, vegetable and animal kingdom, healing, dancing/trance and percussion. Candomblé draws inspiration from a variety of people of the African Diaspora, but it mainly features aspects of Yoruba orisha veneration.

Overview

The Yoruba slaves were referred by various names in the Americas such as Anago, O Lukumi and Nago. In many parts of the Latin America, Orishás are now conflated with Roman Catholic saints. This religion, like many African religions, is an oral tradition and therefore has not been put into text throughout the years. Only recently have scholars and people of this religion begun to write down their practices. The name **Batuque** is also used, especially before the 19th century when *Candomblé* became more common. Both words are believed to derive from a Bantu-family language, mainly that of (Kongo Kingdom).

Candomblé may be called **Macumba** in some regions, notably Rio de Janeiro and São Paulo, although Macumba has a distinct set of practices more akin to European witchcraft. Candomblé can also be distinguished from Umbanda, a religion founded in the early 20th century by combining African elements with Kardecism; and from similar African-derived religions such as Quimbanda, Haitian Vodou, Cuban Santería, and Obeah, which developed independently of Candomblé and are virtually unknown in Brazil.

There are 2 million Candombles worldwide [1].

Nations

Brazilian slaves came from a number of African ethnic groups, including Igbo, Yoruba, Ewe, Fon, and Bantu. Slave handlers classified them by the shore of embarkment, so the relation to their actual ethnicity may be accurate or not. As the religion developed semi-independently in different regions of the country, among different ethnic groups, it evolved into several "sects" or *nations* (*nações*), distinguished chiefly by the set of worshiped deities, as well as the music and language used in the rituals.

Candomblé

The division into nations was also influenced by the religious and beneficent brotherhoods (*irmandades*) of Brazilian slaves organized by the Catholic Church in the 18th and 19th centuries. These fraternities, organized along ethnic lines to allow preaching in the slaves' native languages, provided a legitimate cover for slave reunions, and ultimately may have aided the establishment of Candomblé.

The following list is a rough classification of the major nations and sub-nations, and their sacred languages:

- Ketu or Queto – Yoruba language (*Iorubá* or *Nagô* in Portuguese)
  - *Efã* and *Ijexá* in Bahia
  - *Nagô* or *Eba* in Pernambuco
  - *Oió-ijexá* or *Batuque-de-Nação* in Rio Grande do Sul
  - *Mina-nagô* or *Tambor-de-Mina* in Maranhão
  - *Xambá* in Alagoas and Pernambuco (nearly extinct).
- Bantu or Angola – mix of Bantu (Kikongo and Kimbundo) languages
  - *Caboclo* (A new deity that is the mixture between an Indian and a white European)
- Jeje – Ewe, Fon, and Gen languages (*Jeje*)
  - *Mina Jeje* in Maranhão
  - *Babaçuê* in Pará
  - *Fun Fún* in Panamá

Beliefs

Candomblé is a polytheistic religion and worships a number of gods, derived from African deities:

- the Orishas of Yoruba and Ketashi mythology (Ketu nation), spelled *Orixás* in Portuguese;
- the Voduns of the Ewe and Fon (Jeje nation); and
- the Nkisis (Minkisi) of the Bantu (Angola nation and Congo).
- Tabela Orixas-Voduns-Nkisis [2]

These deities were created by a supreme God: Olodumare, Olorun etc. of the Yoruba, Zambi or Zambiapongo of the Bantu, and Nana Buluku of the Fon.

On the other hand, deities from one nation may be acculturated as "guests" in houses and ceremonies of another nation, besides those of the latter. Some nations assign new names to guest spirits, while some retain the names used in the nation of origin.

Syncretism

There is also an Islamic-linked sect within Candomblé which was more common during the slave days in Brazil. Slaves coming from West Africa had been acculturated with Muslim traditions. These Malês set aside Fridays as the day to worship deities as do the Muslims for prayer and meditation. Malês were the instigators of many slave revolts in Brazil leading in all white with amulets and skull caps as in traditional Islam.

In this regard, it is worth noting that some Candomblé rites have also incorporated local Native American gods — which, to the Church, were just as pagan as the Orixás — because they were seen as the "Orishas of the land". Finally, one should keep in mind that many (if not most) practitioners of Candomblé through the times had not only African roots but European ones as well.

Although syncretism still seems to be prevalent, in recent years the lessening of religious and racial prejudices has given rise to a "traditionalist" movement in Candomblé, that rejects the Christian elements and seeks to recreate a "pure" cult based exclusively in Africa.

Rituals

The Candomblé ritual (*toque*) has two parts: the *preparation*, attended only by priests and initiates, which may start a week in advance; and a festive public "mass" and banquet that starts in the late evening and ends around midnight.

In the first part, initiates and aides wash and iron the costumes for the ceremony, and decorate the house with paper flags and festoons, in the colors favored by the Orixas that are to be honored on that occasion. They also prepare food for the banquet. Some domestic animals are slaughtered; some parts reserved for sacrifice, the rest is prepared for the banquet. On the day of the ceremony, starting in the early morning, cowrie-shell divinations (*jogo de búzios*) are performed, and sacrifices are offered to the desired Orixás, and to the messenger spirit (Exú in Ketu).

In the public part of the ceremony, *children-of-saint* (mediunic priests) invoke and "incorporate" Orixás, falling into a trance-like state. After having fallen into trance, the priest-spirits perform dances symbolic of the Orixá's attributes, while the *babalorixá* or *father of saint* (leading male priest) leads songs that celebrate the spirit's deeds. The ceremony ends with a banquet.

Candomblé music, an essential part of the ritual, derives from African music and has had a strong influence in other popular (non-religious) Brazilian music styles. The word *batuque*, for instance, has entered the Brazilian vernacular as a synonym of "rhythmic percussion music".

Temples and priesthood

Candomblé temples are called *houses* (*casas*), *plantations* (*roças*), or *yards* (*terreiros*). Most Candomblé houses are small, independently owned and managed by the respective higher priests (father- or mother-of-saint). A few of the older and larger houses have a more institutional character and more formal hierarchy. There is no central administration. Inside the place of worship are the altars to the Orixás, or *Pejis*.

Ilê Axé Opó Afonjá

Candomblé priesthood is organized into symbolic *families*, whose members are not necessarily relatives in the common sense. Each *family* owns and manages one *house*. In most houses, especially the larger ones, the head of the *family* is always a woman, the mãe-de-santo, or ialorixá, *mother-of-saint* in Candomblé , seconded by the pais-de-santo, or babalorixá *father-of-saint*.The priests and priestesses may also be known as ialorixá, babalorixá , babalaos (interpreters of búzios), babas, babaloshas,and candomblezeiros. Some houses have a more flexible hierarchy which allows the *father-of-saint* to be the head priest. Often during the slave period, the women became the diviners and healers which was not part of African tradition; however, the male slaves were constantly working and did not have the time to take care of daily instances.

Admission to the priesthood and progression in the hierarchy is conditioned to approval by the Orixás, possession of the necessary qualities, learning the necessary knowledge, and performance of lengthy initiation rites, which last seven years or more. There are generally two types of priesthood in the different nations of Candomble, and they are made up of those who fall in trance by the Orixá (iyawo) and those who do not (Oga – male/Ekeji – female). It is important not to confuse the meaning and usage of the Yoruba term *iyawò* (bride in Yoruba) with other African derived religions that use the same term with different meanings.

The seclusion period for the initiation of an iyawo lasts generally 21 days in the Ketu nation and varies depending on the nation. The iyawo's role in the religion is assigned by a divination made by her/his babalorixá/ialorixá; one function that an iyawo can be assigned for is to take care of neophytes as they in their initiatic seclusion period, becoming an expert in all the Orisa foods, becoming an iya or babalorisa themselves, or knowing all ritual songs, etc... The iyawos follow a 7 years period of apprenticeship within which they offer periodical sacrifices in order to reinforce their initiatic links in the form of the so-called obligations of 1, 3 and 7 years. At the 7th year, the iyawos earn their title and can get a honorific title or religious post (*oye* in Yoruba). Once the iyawo has accomplished their 7th year cycle obligation, they become elders (*egbon* in Yoruba, *egbomi* in Brazil, which means *my elder*) within their religious family.

The other priesthood is reserved for those who do not fall in trance. Ogas and Ekejis do not endure the same path to eldership as do iyawos; they are regarded as elders immediately after their initiation. Their role is to help the baba/ialorixá in different specific ritual tasks like drumming, singing, cooking, taking care of the orixá shrines and when he/she comes down in possession trance, etc... Ogas and Ekejis usually do not go on to become baba/ialorixá, nor do they open their own temples or have *filhos de santo* (they do not initiate others).

Some Well Known Temples in Salvador, Bahia

See also: Olga de Alaketu

- Ketu, Efon and Nago nations

    Nago/Yoruba tradition

    - Ilé Axé Iyá Nassô Oká (Casa Branca do Engenho Velho)
    - Ilé Iyá Omi Axé Iyamassê (Terreiro do Gantois)
    - Ilé Axé Opô Afonjá [3]
    - Ilé Maroialaji (also known as Alaketu)
    - Ilé Axé Oxumarê [4] (male or female leadership)
    - Terreiro do Cobre
    - Asé Yangba Oloroke ti Efon (male or female leadership)
    - Casa de Nago (in São Luís, state of Maranhão)
    - Ilé Axé Obá Ogunté (Sítio do Pai Adão – in Recife, state of Pernambuco)

- Jeje nation

    Ewe-Fon tradition

    - Zoogodô Bogum Male Rundó (Terreiro do Bogum)
    - Casa das Minas (in São Luís, state of Maranhão)
    - Kwe Ceja Unde (Roça do Ventura – City of Cachoeira, state of Bahia)
    - Rumpame Runtoloji (City of Cachoeira, state of Bahia)

Kwé Jidan Vodun Jo

Ilheus

- Mejito Dan Maria de Fatima S. Oliveira (fundadora) 2000
- Angola/Congo nation

    Bantu tradition

    - Manzo Banduquenqué (Bate-Folha)
    - Unzo Tumba Insaba Junçara
    - Unzo Nkisi Tombensi

Upon the death of an ialorixá, the successor is chosen, usually among her "filhas-de-santo", usually by means of divination using consecrated cowrie shells that are considered to be the mouthpieces of the Orixa cowrie shell. However the succession may be very disputed or may fail to find a successor, and often leads to splitting or closing down of the *house*. In some terreiros (like Gantois, Alaketu, Terreiro do Cobre and now, the Oxumarê), the leadership is inherited by a late ialorixá's female blood relative (usually one of her own daughters). Only a handful of *houses* in Brazil have seen their 100th anniversary. Among the oldest that are still existent are *Ilé Axé Iyá Nassô Oká* (literally, "White House at the Old Sugarmill"), in Salvador, Bahia, and the *Casa das Minas* in São Luís, Maranhão (ca. 1796).

Priesthood Initiation

In Brazil: Ifá, Egungun, Orisha (Orixa), Vodun and Nkisi, are separated by type of priesthood initiation.

- Ifá only initiation Babalawos, do not come into trance.
- Egungun only initiation Babaojés, do not come into trance.
- Candomblé Ketu initiation Iyawos, come into trance with Orixá.
- Candomblé Jeje initiation Vodunsis, come into trance with Vodun.
- Candomblé Bantu initiation Muzenzas, come into trance with Nkisi.

Priesthood

In Afro-Brazilian Religion the priesthood is divided into:

- Babalorixá or Iyalorixá – Priest's Orixás
- Doté or Doné – Priest's Voduns
- Tateto or Mameto – Priest's Nkisis
- Babalawo – Priest's Orunmila-Ifa, Worship of Ifá
- Bokonon – Priest's Vodun Fa
- BabalOsanyin – Priest's Osanyin
- Babaojé – Priest's Worship the Egungun

See also

- Candomblé Jejé
- Candomblé Ketu
- Candomblé Bantu
- Gerard Béhague, candomblé music expert

Books

- Bastide, Roger. *Le candomblé de Bahia* . 2001, Paris, Plon.
- Bramley, Serge. *Macumba*. 1994 – City Lights Books.
- Brown, Diana. Umbanda: Religion and Politics in Urban Brazil. 1994 – Columbia University Press.
- Capone, Stefania. Searching for Africa in Brazil. Power and Tradition in Candomblé . Duke University Press, 2010.
- Carneiro, Edison. "The Structure of African Cults in Bahia" Civilzacao Brasileira, Rio De Janeiro. 1936–37.
- Gordon, Jacob U. " Yoruba Cosmology And Culture in Brazil: A Study of African Survivals in the New World." Journal of Black Studies, Vol.10, No 2. (December 1979): P. 231- 244
- Herkovits, Melville J. "The Social Organization of the Afrobrazilian Candomble." *Proceedings of the Congress* São Paulo, 1955.
- Johnson, Paul Christopher. "Secrets, Gossip, and Gods The Transformation of Brazilian Candomblé". 2002 – Oxford University Press.
- Landes, Ruth. The City of Women. 1994 – University of New Mexico Press.
- Matory, J. Lorand. Black Atlantic Religion: Tradition, Transnationalism, and Matriarchy in the Afro-Brazillian Candomblé . 2005 – Princeton University Press.
- Matory, J. Lorand. "Gendered Agendas: The Secrets Scholars Keep about Yoruba-Atlantic Religion." Gender & History 15, no. 3 (November 2003): p. 409–439."
- Omari-Tunkara, Mikelle S. "Manipulating the Sacred: Yoruba Art, Ritual, and Resistance in Brazilian Candomble". 2005 – Wayne State University Press.
- Reis, João José. "Candomblé in Nineteenth-Century Bahia: Priests, Followers, Clients" in *Rethinking the African Diaspora:The Making of a Black Atlantic World in the Bight of Benin and Brazil* Mann, Kristina and Bay, Edna G. Ed. Geu Heuman and James Walvin. 2001-Frank Cass
- Reis, João José. *Slave Rebellion in Brazil:The Muslim Uprising of 1835 in Bahia* (Baltimore and London:The Johns Hopkins University Press,1995).
- Souty, Jérôme. *Pierre Fatumbi Verger: Du Regard Détaché à la Connaissance Initiatique*, Paris, Maisonneuve & Larose, 2007.
- Voeks, Robert A. "Sacred Leaves of Candomble: African Magic, Medicine, and Religion in Brazil." Austin, TX: University of Texas Press, 1997.
- Verger, Pierre Fatumbi. "Dieux D'Afrique. Paul Hartmann, Paris (1st edition, 1954; 2nd edition, 1995). 400pp, 160 b/w photos, ISBN 2-909571-13-0.
- McGowan, Chris and Pessanha, Ricardo. "The Brazilian Sound: Samba, Bossa Nova and the Popular Music of Brazil." 1998. 2nd edition. Temple University Press. ISBN 1-56639-545-3
- Wafer, Jim. Taste of Blood: Spirit Possession in Brazilian Candomble. 1991 – University of Pennsylvania Press.

External links

- Candomblé music [5] Webcast explores the influence of African culture on Brazilian music
- Federação Internacional de Umbanda e Candomblé [6]
- Ilé Axé Opô Afonjá, a major *house* [7]
- Ama, A Story of the Atlantic Slave Trade [8]
- Unesco 2004: Slavery Abolition Year [9]

Portuguese

- Extensive info on the Orixás [10]
- Candomblé information – includes lexicons of Candomblé sacred languages [11]
- Orixá imagery [12]

French

- Prefaces of Berger's book [13]

English

- Quimbanda Web page – Brazilian Tradition related to Candomble [14]
- Candomblé in Salvador da Bahia [15]
- Baba Alawoye.com [16] Baba'Awo Awoyinfa Ifaloju, using web media 2.0 (blogs, podcasting, video & photocasting)

Cartomancy

Cartomancy is fortune-telling or divination using a deck of cards. Forms of cartomancy appeared soon after playing cards were first introduced into Europe in the 14th century. Practitioners of cartomancy are generally known as *cartomancers*, *card readers* or, simply, *readers*. Wikipedia:Avoid weasel wordsSome practitioners have claimed that cartomancy's origins date back to ancient Egyptian times.[*citation needed*]

The Fortune Teller, by Art Nouveau painter Mikhail Vrubel, depicting a cartomancer

Cartomancy using standard playing cards was the most popular form of providing "fortune telling" card readings in the 18th, 19th and 20th centuries. In English-speaking countries, a standard deck of Anglo-American bridge/poker playing cards (i.e., 52-card, four suit set) can be used in the cartomancy reading; the deck is often augmented with jokers, and even with the blank card found in many packaged decks. In France, the 32-card piquet playing card deck was, and still is, most typically used in cartomancy readings, while the 52-card deck was, and still is, also used for this purpose. (For a piquet deck, start with a 52-card deck and remove all of the 2s through the 6s. This leaves all of the 7s through the 10s, the face cards, and the aces.)

In recent years, however, the popularity of Tarot readings has diminished to a certain degree the popularity of the once-common cartomancy readings using standard playing cards.[*citation needed*]

According to some, a deck that is used for cartomancy should not be used for any other purpose. Cartomancers generally feel that the deck should be treated as a tool and cared for accordingly. Some cartomancers also feel that the cards should never be touched by anyone other than their owner.

Methods of cartomancy

Although a standard playing card deck can be used for cartomancy, other decks are used such as tarot decks. In the view of some, including the webmaster of the Aeclectic Tarot website [1], any deck that is not a tarot deck (56 minor arcana with 4 suits of 14 cards and 22 major arcana) is referred to, more generally, as a *cartomancy deck*.

The Tarot deck differs somewhat from the standard deck used for cartomancy. The Tarot deck consists of twenty-one "trump" cards and a "Fool" card, these being referred to collectively by occultists as Major Arcana, and fifty-six conventional cards, called the Minor Arcana (Arcana means "hidden things"). Each Minor Arcana suit contains four court cards (usually king, queen, knight and page) along with the usual ten numbered, or pip, cards.

French suited Playing Card and Latin suited Tarot Equivalents:

- Clubs = Sticks or wands (power) Fire element Salamander
- Diamonds = Coins or mirrors, aka Pentacles (health; material matters) Earth element Gnome
- Hearts = Cups (emotions) Water element Undine
- Spades = Swords (intellect; education) Air element Sylph
- Tears = Waves (aging, experience) Wood element Fae
- Hands = Groups of people (togetherness) Metal element Dwarf

   The suits "Swords" and "Wands" are disputed between cartomancers.

Criticism

The interpretations of the meanings of different cards even within the same deck varies greatly among cartomancers. This raises doubt in the idea that there is some objective message coming directly from the cards, as might necessary for amateur cartomancers to derive use from them. While most parapsychologists would argue that the card reader's psi faculties ought to play a significant role in determining both how the cards land and how they are interpreted [*citation needed*] - making the lack of an objective standard irrelevant *stricto sensu* - the lack of a shared understanding of card meanings clearly hinders both verification of cartomancy's effectiveness and communication between practitioners.

Cartomancy has also been criticized for not providing a proposed physical mechanism by which cards could be used to predict one's future. Additionally, there have been no tests to date that show that cartomancy does any better than chance in either predicting the future or determining traits about individuals, despite large incentives to cartomancers who can show a successful test, such as the Randi challenge.[*citation needed*]

Divination techniques such as cartomancy are forbidden within Christianity and Judaism: - "Ye shall not... use enchantment, nor observe times." -Leviticus 19:26. - "Ye shall not... practise divination nor soothsaying." - Lev. xix. 26

See also
- Tarot reading
- Oracle card decks
- Marie Anne Lenormand (1772–1843)

Clairvoyance

Terminology	
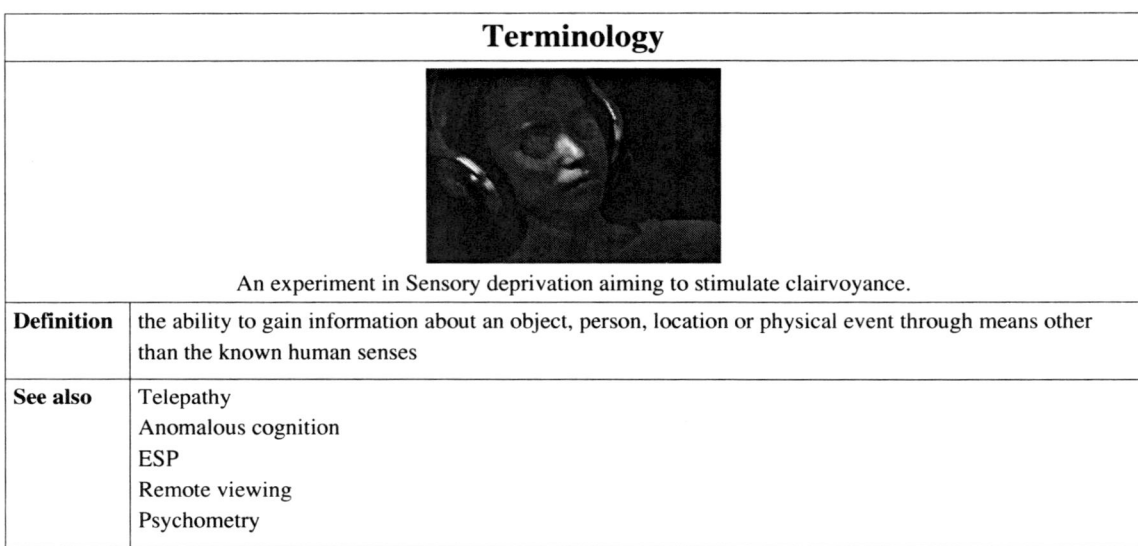 An experiment in Sensory deprivation aiming to stimulate clairvoyance.	
Definition	the ability to gain information about an object, person, location or physical event through means other than the known human senses
See also	Telepathy Anomalous cognition ESP Remote viewing Psychometry

The term **clairvoyance** (from 17th century French with *clair* meaning "clear" and *voyance* meaning "vision") is used to refer to the ability to gain information about an object, person, location or physical event through means other than the known human senses, a form of extra-sensory perception. A person said to have the ability of clairvoyance is referred to as a **clairvoyant** ("one who sees clearly").

Claims for the existence of paranormal and psychic abilities such as clairvoyance are highly controversial. Parapsychology explores this possibility, but the existence of the paranormal is generally not accepted by the scientific community.

Usage

Within parapsychology, clairvoyance is used exclusively to refer to the transfer of information that is both contemporary to, and hidden from, the clairvoyant. It is very different from telepathy in that the information is said to be gained directly from an external physical source, rather than being transferred from the mind of one individual to another.

Outside of parapsychology, clairvoyance is often used to refer to other forms of anomalous cognition, most commonly the perception of events that have occurred in the past, or which will occur in the future (known as retrocognition and precognition respectively), or to refer to communications with the dead (see Mediumship).

Clairvoyance is related to remote viewing, although the term "remote viewing" itself is not as widely applicable to clairvoyance because it refers to a specific controlled process.

(Bruce Main-Smith writes):- It is unfortunate, indeed careless, that clairvoyance has come to be indicative of all/most forms of purported mediumship. There are four primary channels, clairsensing, trance, healing and physical plus a whole raft of others that do not fit neatly into any one primary channel. Clairvoyance (seeing) and clairaudience (hearing) for example are both kinds of clairsensing and belong in that main group. Many mediums who are good clairvoyants may well have little or no clairaudient capability even though both "gifts" belong in the primary channel of clairsensing. Remote viewing is a facet of clairvoyance and usually appears in practitioners suffering from arrested development.

Trance is the ability to communicate with, and mainly to receive from, other entities, incarnate & discarnate, and may sometimes be independent of time; it is usually divided into deep trance (obliterative & so dangerous, where the operative abdicates the throne, quite common) and light trance (a high or even total degree of awareness & thus safer for the practitioner, and extremely rare when well-done).

Healing is the ability to induct health benefits from some usually unspecified higher source where the healer can direct the effects to the beneficiary. Contact healing involves the healer being in the closest proximity but not necessarily actually touching. Absent healing is explained by its alternative name of distant healing and is independent of spatial distance.

Physical mediumship includes events such as table turning, production of quasi-physical objects (even personages) & sometimes involving so-called ectoplasm. It is often said to require either total darkness or at the most a weak red light.

There are many further mediumistic events, still unfortunately too often dubbed clairvoyance, which do not fit neatly into any of the four main channels. These include psychometry (establishing the history of an object), slate writing (common in Victorian times), extras appearing in photographs (seemingly no more; possibly since the advent of compound camera lenses using plastic as well as quartz-glass) and a long list of other curiosities too extensive to be dealt with here.

It is most unusual for a medium to have more than one primary channel "open" and under control.

Status of clairvoyance

Within the field of parapsychology, there is a consensus that some instances of clairvoyance are verifiable. There is also a measured level of belief from amongst the general public, within a portion of the US population who believe in clairvoyance varying between 1/4 and 1/3 over the 15 year period from 1990 to 2005.

Year	Belief
1990	26%
2000	32%
2005	26%

The concept of clairvoyance gained some support from the US and Russian governments both during and after the Cold War, and both governments made several attempts to harness it as an intelligence gathering tool.

According to skeptics, clairvoyance is the result of fraud, self-delusion, Barnum effects, confirmatory biases, or failures to appreciate the base rate of chance occurrences. For example, in a scientific experiment of clairvoyance, a purported clairvoyant participant will inevitably make correct guesses some of the time (i.e., during some of the trials within the same experiment), simply because of chance. Furthermore, because of the nature of the statistical tests used by experimenters, a very small proportion of all experiments conducted will yield an overall statistically significant result (suggesting that clairvoyance took place at above-chance levels), again simply because of chance. A proper summary of the experimental evidence on clairvoyance should include a summary of all experiments that were conducted, taking into account their probabilities of turning out false positive and false negative results, and making sure that studies are not included in the review selectively. Some researchers on clairvoyance have tended to purposefully exclude negative findings from their reviews , thus biasing their own conclusions.

Clairvoyance and related phenomena throughout history

There have been anecdotal reports of clairvoyance and 'clear' abilities throughout history in most cultures. Often clairvoyance has been associated with religious or shamanic figures, offices and practices. For example, ancient Hindu religious texts list clairvoyance amongst other forms of 'clear' experiencing, as siddhis, or 'perfections', skills that are yielded through appropriate meditation and personal discipline. But a large number of anecdotal accounts of clairvoyance are of the spontaneous variety among the general populace. For example, many people report seeing a loved one who has recently died before they have learned by other means that their loved one is deceased. While anecdotal accounts do not provide scientific proof of clairvoyance, such common experiences continue to motivate research into such phenomena.

The earliest record of somnambulistic clairvoyance is credited to the Marquis de Puységur, a follower of Mesmer, who in 1784 was treating a local dull-witted peasant named Victor Race. During treatment, Race reportedly would go into trance and undergo a personality change, becoming fluent and articulate, and giving diagnosis and prescription for his own disease as well as those of others. When he came out of the trance state he would be unaware of anything he had said or done. This behavior is somewhat reminiscent of the reported behaviors of the 20th century medical clairvoyant and psychic Edgar Cayce. It is reported that although Puységur used the term 'clairvoyance', he did not think of these phenomena as "paranormal", since he accepted mesmerism as one of the natural sciences.

Clairvoyance was a reported ability of some mediums during the spiritualist period of the late 19th and early 20th centuries, and psychics of many descriptions have claimed clairvoyant ability up to the present day.

Early researchers of clairvoyance included William Gregory (chemist), Gustav Pagenstecher, and Rudolf Tischner. These were largely qualitative experiments in which selected participants sought to identify a concealed target image, or to provide accurate information about the history of a target object. Charles Richet, the noted physiologist and, later, Ina Jephson, a member of the Society for Psychical Research, introduced more quantitative methods. A significant development in clairvoyance research came when J. B. Rhine, a psychologist at Duke University, introduced a standard methodology, with a standard statistical approach to analysing the data, as part of his research into extrasensory perception. Perhaps the best-known study of clairvoyance in recent times has been the US government-funded remote viewing project at SRI/SAIC during the 1970s through the mid-1990s; at least those studies amongst these that did not involve "agents" visiting or being otherwise aware of the target sites.

Some parapsychologists have proposed that our different functional labels (clairvoyance, telepathy, precognition, etc.) all refer to one basic underlying mechanism, although there is not yet any satisfactory theory for what that mechanism may be.[citation needed]

Parapsychological research

Parapsychological research studies of remote viewing and clairvoyance have produced favorable results significantly above chance, and meta-analysis of these studies increases the significance. For instance, at the Stanford Research Institute, in 1972, Harold Puthoff and Russell Targ initiated a series of human subject studies to determine whether participants (the *viewers* or *percipients*) could reliably identify and accurately describe salient features of remote locations or *targets*. In the early studies, a human *sender* was typically present at the remote location, as part of the experiment protocol. A three-step process was used, the first step being to randomly select the target conditions to be experienced by the senders. Secondly, in the viewing step, participants were asked to verbally express or sketch their impressions of the remote scene. Thirdly, in the judging step, these descriptions were matched by separate judges, as closely as possible, with the intended targets. The term remote viewing was coined to describe this overall process.

Targ and Puthoff both believed that Uri Geller, retired police commissioner Pat Price and artist Ingo Swann all had genuine psychic abilities. They published their findings in *Nature* and the *Proceedings of the IEEE*. Their work however met criticism from a number of writers, such as psychologists David Marks and Richard Kammann in their 1980 book *The Psychology of the Psychic*.

In order to explore the nature of remote viewing channel, the viewer in some experiments was secured in a double-walled copper-screened Faraday cage. Although this provided attenuation of radio signals over a broad range of frequencies, the researchers found that it did not alter the subject's remote viewing capability. They postulated that extremely low frequency (ELF) propagation might be involved, since Faraday cage screening is less effective in the ELF range. Such a hypothesis had previously been put forward by telepathy researchers in the Soviet Union.

The first paper by Puthoff and Targ on psychic research to appear in a mainstream peer-reviewed scientific journal was published in Nature in March 1974; in it, the team reported some degree of remote viewing success. One of the individuals involved in these initial studies at SRI was Uri Geller, a well-known celebrity psychic at the time. The research team reported witnessing some of Geller's trademark metal spoon-bending performances, but admitted that they were unable to conduct adequately controlled experiments to confirm any paranormal hypothesis about them.

Electroencephalography (EEG) techniques were also used by team to examine ESP phenomena. In these investigations, a sender, who was isolated in a visually opaque, electrically and acoustically shielded chamber, was stimulated at random by bursts of strobe-light flickers The experimenters reported that, for one receiver, differential alpha block on control and stimulus trials were observed, which showed that some information transfer had occurred. In contrast, this person's expressed statements of when the stimulus occurred were no different than that which would be expected by chance. The researches were unable to identify the physical parameters by which the EEG effect was mediated.

After the publication of these findings, various attempts to replicate the remote viewing findings were quickly carried out. Several of these follow-up studies, which involved viewing in group settings, reported some limited success. They included the use of face-to-face groups, and remotely-linked groups using computer conferencing.

The various debates in the mainstream scientific literature prompted the editors of 'Proceedings of the IEEE' to invite Robert Jahn, then Dean of the School of Engineering at Princeton University, to write a comprehensive review of psychic phenomena from an engineering perspective. His paper, published in February 1982, includes numerous references to remote viewing replication studies at the time.

Clairvoyance experiments involving Zener cards currently exist on the internet. One such online system, the Anima Project, gathers user results into a master database which is then analyzed using a variety of statistical techniques.

Skepticism

Parapsychological research is regarded by critics as a pseudoscience In 1988, the US National Research Council concluded that it "...finds no scientific justification from research conducted over a period of 130 years, for the existence of parapsychological phenomena."

Skeptics say that if clairvoyance were a reality it would have become abundantly clear. They also contend that those who believe in paranormal phenomena do so for merely psychological reasons. According to David G. Myers (*Psychology*, 8th ed.)

> The search for a valid and reliable test of clairvoyance has resulted in thousands of experiments. One controlled procedure has invited 'senders' to telepathically transmit one of four visual images to 'receivers' deprived of sensation in a nearby chamber (Bem & Honorton, 1994). The result? A reported 32 percent accurate response rate, surpassing the chance rate of 25 percent. But follow-up studies have (depending on who was summarizing the results) failed to replicate the phenomenon or produced mixed results (Bem & others, 2001; Milton & Wiseman, 2002; Storm, 2000, 2003).
>
> One skeptic, magician James Randi, has a longstanding offer—now U.S. $1 million—"to anyone who proves a genuine psychic power under proper observing conditions" (Randi, 1999). French, Australian, and Indian groups have parallel offers of up to 200,000 euros to anyone with demonstrable paranormal abilities (CFI, 2003). Large as these sums are, the scientific seal of approval would be worth far more to anyone whose claims could be authenticated. To refute those who say there is no ESP, one need only produce a single person who can demonstrate a single, reproducible ESP phenomenon. So far, no such person has emerged. Randi's offer has been publicized for three decades and dozens of people have been tested, sometimes under the scrutiny of an independent panel of judges. Still, nothing. "People's desire to believe in the paranormal is stronger than all the evidence that it does not exist." Susan Blackmore, "Blackmore's first law", 2004.

Other related terms

The words "clairvoyance" and "psychic" are often used to refer to many different kinds of paranormal sensory experiences, but there are more specific names:

Clairsentience (feeling/touching)

In the field of parapsychology, **clairsentience** is a form of extra-sensory perception wherein a person acquires psychic knowledge primarily by feeling. The word is from the French clair, "clear," + sentience, "feeling," and is ultimately derived from the Latin clarus, "clear," + sentiens, derived from sentire, "to feel".

In addition to parapsychology, the term also plays a role in some religions. For example: clairsentience is one of the six human special functions mentioned or recorded in Buddhism. It is an ability that can be obtained at advanced meditation level. Generally the term refers to a person who can feel the vibration of other people. There are many different degrees of clairsentience ranging from the perception of diseases of other people to the thoughts or emotions of other people. The ability differs from third eye in that this kind of ability cannot have a vivid picture in the mind. Instead, a very vivid feeling can form.

Psychometry is related to clairsentience. The word stems from *psyche* and *metric*, which means "soul-measuring".

Clairaudience (hearing/listening)

In the field of parapsychology, **clairaudience** [from late 17th century French *clair* (clear) & audience (hearing)] is a form of extra-sensory perception wherein a person acquires information by paranormal auditory means. It is often considered to be a form of clairvoyance. Clairaudience is essentially the ability to hear in a paranormal manner, as opposed to paranormal seeing (clairvoyance) and feeling (clairsentience). Clairaudient people have psi-mediated hearing. Clairaudience may refer not to actual perception of sound, but may instead indicate impressions of the "inner mental ear" similar to the way many people think words without having auditory impressions. But it may also refer to actual perception of sounds such as voices, tones, or noises which are not apparent to other humans or to recording equipment. For instance, a clairaudient person might claim to hear the voices or thoughts of the spirits of persons who are deceased. In Buddhism, it is believed that those who have extensively practiced Buddhist meditation and have reached a higher level of consciousness can activate their "third ear" and hear the music of the spheres; i.e. the music of the celestial gandharvas. Clairaudience may be positively distinguished from the voices heard by the mentally ill when it reveals information unavailable to the clairaudient person by normal means (including cold reading or other magic tricks), and thus may be termed "psychic" or paranormal.[*citation needed*]

Clairalience (smelling)

Also known as Clairescence. In the field of parapsychology, **clairalience** [presumably from late 17th century French *clair* (clear) & alience (smelling)] is a form of extra-sensory perception wherein a person accesses psychic knowledge through the physical sense of smell.

Claircognizance (knowing)

In the field of parapsychology, **claircognizance** [presumably from late 17th century French *clair* (clear) & *cognizance* (< ME *cognisaunce* < OFr *conoissance*, knowledge)] is a form of extra-sensory perception wherein a person acquires psychic knowledge primarily by means of intrinsic knowledge. It is the ability to know something without a physical explanation why you know it, like the concept of mediums.

Clairgustance (tasting)

In the field of parapsychology, **clairgustance** is defined as a form of extra-sensory perception that allegedly allows one to taste a substance without putting anything in one's mouth. It is claimed that those who possess this ability are able to perceive the essence of a substance from the spiritual or ethereal realms through taste.[citation needed]

See also

Part of a series of articles on the paranormal
Main articles
Paranormal · Supernatural · Occult · Forteana · Miracle · Magic · Aura · Ghost · Ghost hunting · Ghost story · Fear of ghosts · Poltergeist · Cold spot · Haunted locations: World, United States, United Kingdom · Haunted house · Intelligent haunting · Residual haunting · Electronic voice phenomenon · Spirit photography · Ectoplasm · Shadow people · Will-o'-the-wisp · Spirit possession · Demonic possession · Demon · Demonology · Exorcism · Paranormal television · Paranormal fiction · Afterlife · Reincarnation · Spirit world · Spiritualism · Ouija · Conjuration · Clairvoyance · Mediumship · Psychic · Psychic reading · Remote viewing · Extra-sensory perception · Precognition · Near-death experience · Psychometry · Psychokinesis · Hypnosis · Telepathy · Parapsychology · Close encounter · Ufology · UFO · UFO sightings · Paranormal and occult UFO hypotheses · Cryptozoology · Cryptid
Articles on skepticism
Scientific skepticism · Hoax · Pseudoskepticism · Debunking · Cold reading · Magical thinking · Challenges for paranormal evidence · Committee for Skeptical Inquiry · James Randi Educational Foundation
Related articles on science, psychology, and logic
Anomalistics · Scientific method · Falsifiability · Pseudoscience · Fringe science · Protoscience · Fallacy · Argument from ignorance · Agnosticism · Uncertainty
Related articles on Social change and Parapsychology
Countermovement · Social movement · Death and culture · Parapsychology

- Channeling (mediumistic)
- Anomalous cognition
- Astral projection
- List of parapsychology topics
- Near-death experience
- Out-of-body experience
- Paranormal phenomena
- Parapsychology
- Plane (esotericism)

- Postdiction (retroactive clairvoyance)
- Precognition
- Spirituality
- Subtle body
- Third eye
- Schizophrenia
- Visionary

Further reading

- "All that clairvoyant stuff – I don't see it myself: A new law against mediums would not work" [1] by Daniel Finkelstein, *The Times*, April 11, 2007.
- *Mental Radio* by Upton Sinclair, 1929. Preface by Albert Einstein.

Collective unconscious

Part of a series of articles on
Psychoanalysis

Psychology portal

Collective unconscious is a term of analytical psychology, coined by Carl Jung. It is proposed to be a part of the unconscious mind, expressed in humanity and all life forms with nervous systems, and describes how the structure of the psyche autonomously organizes experience. Jung distinguished the collective unconscious from the personal unconscious, in that the personal unconscious is a personal reservoir of experience unique to each individual, while the collective unconscious collects and organizes those personal experiences in a similar way with each member of a particular species.

For Jung, "My thesis then, is as follows: in addition to our immediate consciousness, which is of a thoroughly personal nature and which we believe to be the only empirical psyche (even if we tack on the personal unconscious as an appendix), there exists a second psychic system of a collective, universal, and impersonal nature which is identical in all individuals. This collective unconscious does not develop individually but is inherited. It consists of pre-existent forms, the archetypes, which can only become conscious secondarily and which give definite form to certain psychic contents.".

Jung also made reference to contents of this category of the unconscious psyche as being similar to Levy-Bruhl's use of *collective representations* or "représentations collectives," Mythological "motifs," Hubert and Mauss's "categories of the imagination," and Adolf Bastian's "primordial thoughts."

Jung's writing style has often been described as dense and technical, which might have contributed to the definition of the collective unconscious being misconstrued as an inheritance of accumulated experience from preceding generations.Wikipedia:No original research

See also

- Archetype
- 8-Circuit Model of Consciousness (7th circuit)
- Evolutionary psychology
- Hippocampus
- Precognition
- Collective consciousness (sociology)
- Depth psychology

Further reading

- Jung, Carl. (1959). *Archetypes and the Collective Unconscious.*
- Jung, Carl. *The Development of Personality.*
- Jung, Carl. (1970). "Psychic conflicts in a child.", *Collected Works of C. G. Jung, 17*. Princeton University Press. 235 p. (p. 1-35).
- Whitmont, Edward C. (1969). *The Symbolic Quest.* Princeton University Press.
- Gallo, Ernest. "Synchronicity and the Archetypes," *Skeptical Inquirer, 18* (4). Summer 1994.

External links

- for Research in Archetypal Symbolism [1] A pictorial and written archive of mythological, ritualistic, and symbolic images from all over the world and from all epochs of human history.
- Kaleidoscope Forum [2] Jungian Discussion Forum. All levels of discourse welcomed.

Coven

A **coven** or **covan** is a name used to describe a gathering of witches or in some cases vampires. Due to the word's association with witches, a gathering of Wiccans, followers of the witchcraft-based neopagan religion of Wicca, is also described as a coven.

The word was originally a late medieval Scots word (circa 1500) meaning a gathering of any kind, according to the Oxford English Dictionary. It derives from the Latin root word *convenire* meaning to come together or to gather, which also gave rise to the English word *convene*. The first recorded use of it being applied to witches comes much later, from 1662 in the witch-trial of Isobel Gowdie, which describes a coven of 13 members.

The word *coven* remained largely unused in English until 1921 when Margaret Murray promoted the idea, now much disputed, that all witches across Europe met in groups of thirteen which they called 'covens'.

The coven in Neopaganism

In Wicca and other similar forms of modern neopagan witchcraft, such as Stregheria and Feri Witchcraft, a coven is a gathering or community of witches, much like a congregation in Christian parlance. It is composed of a group of believers who gather together for ceremonies of worship such as Drawing Down the Moon, or celebrating the Sabbats. The number of persons involved may vary. Although thirteen has been suggestedWikipedia:Avoid weasel words as the optimum number (probably in deference to Murray's theories), any number above and including three can be a coven.[*citation needed*] Two would usually be referred to as a working couple (in any combination of sexes.) Within the community, many believe that a coven larger than thirteen is unwieldy, citing unwieldy group dynamics and an unfair burden on the leadership. When a coven has grown too large to be manageable, it may split, or "hive". In Wicca this may also occur when a newly made High Priest or High Priestess, also called 3rd Degree ordination, leaves to start their own coven. Wiccan covens are generally jointly led by a High Priestess and a High Priest, though some are led by only one or the other. In more recent forms of neopagan witchcraft, covens are sometimes run as democracies with a rotating leadership.

Online covens

With the rise of the World Wide Web as a platform for collaborative discussion and media dissemination, it became popular for adherents and practitioners of Wicca to establish (often paid subscription-based) "online covens" which remotely teach tradition-specific crafts to students in a similar method of education as non-religious virtual online schools.

One of the first online covens to take this route is the Coven of the Far Flung Net, which was established in 1998 as the online arm of the Church of Universal Eclectic Wicca.

However, because of potentially-unwieldy membership sizes, many online covens limit their memberships to anywhere between 10 to 100 students. The CFFN, in particular, tried to devolve its structure into a system of sub-coven clans (which governed their own application processes), a system which ended in 2003 due to fears by the CFFN leadership that the clans were becoming communities in their own right.

Covens in literature and popular culture

An intermediate view is often portrayed in fantasy stories and popular culture. In this usage, a coven is a gathering of witches to work spells in tandem. Such imagery can be traced back to Renaissance prints depicting witches and to the three 'weird sisters' in Shakespeare's play Macbeth. More orgiastic witches' meetings are also depicted in Robert Burns' poem Tam o' Shanter and in Goethe's play Faust. Movie portrayals have included, for example, *Suspiria*, *Rosemary's Baby*, *The Covenant*, *Underworld* and *Underworld: Evolution*, *The Craft* and *COVEN*. In television, covens were portrayed in the U.S. supernatural drama, *Charmed*.

Vampire covens

'Coven' can be a term used to describe a group or community of Sanguinarians, especially those who communicate only over the internet. It almost certainly derives from Wiccan usage of the term. The concept of vampire covens has appeared in the novels of *Anne Rice* and in later horror and fantasy literature such as *Twilight*.

References

- *Drawing Down the Moon* Margot Adler (Penguin Books; 2006)
- *The Spiral Dance* Miriam Simos (HarperSanFrancisco, 1999)
- *A Witches' Bible: The Complete Witches Handbook* Janet and Stuart Farrar (Phoenix Publishing, 1996)

External links

- List of Covens by Location [1] at Witchvox
- Online Covens [2] supported by SpellsOfMagic
- Choosing a Coven [3] by Judy Harrow
- Choosing a Coven [4] (advice on) by Lisa Mc Sherry

Charmstone

A **charmstone** is a mineral specimen believed by adherents of certain cultural or religions traditions to have healing, mystical or paranormal powers or energy. The mineral specimen can be either natural and complete or cleaved from a natural stone; in some cases, the article may be entirely manufactured as in the case of certain Mayan pottery finds. For example, the Miwok and Pomo tribes of Northern California have left thousands of charmstones in the bed of Tolay Lake in Sonoma County. Charmstones are evidenced by the Shalagram and lingam in the Hindu tradition and by maban in the indigenous Australian tradition. The worship of the Black Stone as a charmstone is of particular importance to Islam. Jigme Lingpa in the Vajrayana tradition wrote a treatise on charmstone usage which Namkhai Norbu mentions. Charmstones were used in prehistoric Native American ceremonies for broad spiritual purposes including securing of productive harvests. Today charmstones remain very popular among certain subcultures within Western society, such as the New Age movement, particularly in the form of crystal healing. However, belief in the powers of charmstones is criticized as baseless by scientists and medical professionals who point out that there is no known scientific basis for a crystal healing effect.

Quartz crystal

References

- A Charmstone Discovery in the Redwood Forests of Mendocino County, California [1] by: Susan M. Hector, Daniel G. Foster, Linda C. Pollack Gerrit L. Fenenga, and J. Charles Whatford of the California Department of Forestry and Fire Protection , Archaeology Office. November 30, 2005
- Campbell, Dan, *Edgar Cayce, on the Power of Color, Stones, and Crystals*, Warner Books Edition, New York, NY, 1989.
- Helwig, David, *Crystal Healing* in *Encyclopedia of Alternative Medicine*, 2006 [2]

External links

- Skeptic's Dictionary on Crystal Power [3]

Chakra

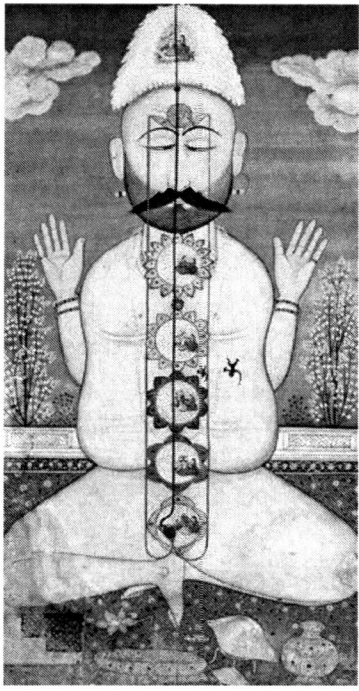

Chakras in the human body depicted with their residing deities.

This article contains Indic text. Without proper rendering support, you may see question marks or boxes, misplaced vowels or missing conjuncts instead of Indic text.

Chakra (derived from the Sanskrit *cakraṃ* चक्रं (['tʃəkrə̃]), pronounced Hindustani pronunciation: ['tʃəkrə] in Hindi; Pali: *chakka* च्हक्क, Tamil: Sakkeram, Chinese: 轮, Tibetan: ▯▯▯▯▯▯▯; *khorlo*) is a Sanskrit word that translates as "wheel" or "turning".

Chakra is a concept referring to wheel-like vortices which, according to traditional Indian medicine, are believed to exist in the surface of the etheric double of man. The Chakras are said to be "force centers" or whorls of energy permeating, from a point on the physical body, the layers of the subtle bodies in an ever-increasing fan-shaped formation. Rotating vortices of subtle matter, they are considered the focal points for the reception and transmission of energies. Different systems posit a varying number of chakras, the most well known system in the West is that of 7 chakras.

It is typical for chakras to be depicted as either flower-like or wheel-like. In the former, a specific number of "petals" are shown around the perimeter of a circle. In the latter, a certain number of spokes divide the circle into segments that make the chakra resemble a wheel (or "chakra"). Each chakra possesses a specific number of segments or petals.

Texts documenting the chakras go back as far as the later Upanishads, for example the Yoga Kundalini Upanishad.

Definitions

Although there are various different interpretations as to what exactly a chakra is, the following features are common in all systems:

- They form part of a subtle energy body, along with the energy channels, or nadis, and the subtle winds, or pranas.
- They are located along a central nadi, Sushumna, which runs either alongside or inside the spine.
- Two other nadis, Ida and Pingala, also run through the chakras, and alongside Sushumna. They occasionally cross Sushumna at the location of the chakras.
- They possess a number of 'petals' or 'spokes'. In some traditions, such as the Tibetan, these spokes branch off into the thousands of nadis that run throughout the human body.
- They are generally associated with a mantra seed-syllable, and often with a variety of colours and deities.

Paramhans Swami Maheshwarananda describes a chakra as:

Sapta Chakra, from a Yoga manuscript in Braj Bhasa language with 118 pages. 1899.

> ...[a] powerhouse in the way it generates and stores energy, with the energy from cosmos pulled in more strongly at these points. The main nadis, Ida, Pingala and Shushumna (sympathetic, parasympathetic, and central nervous system) run along the spinal column in a curved path and cross one another several times. At the points of intersection they form strong energy centers known as chakras. In the human body there are three types of energy centers. The lower or animal chakras are located in the region between the toes and the pelvic region indicating our evolutionary origins in the animal kingdom. The human chakras lie along the spinal column. Finally, the higher or divine Chakras are found between the top of the spine and the crown of the head.

Anodea Judith (1996: p. 5) provides a modern interpretation of the chakras:

Chakra

> A chakra is believed to be a center of activity that receives, assimilates, and expresses life force energy. The word *chakra* literally translates as *wheel* or *disk* and refers to a spinning sphere of bioenergetic activity emanating from the major nerve ganglia branching forward from the spinal column. Generally, six of these wheels are described, stacked in a column of energy that spans from the base of the spine to the middle of the forehead, the seventh lying beyond the physical world. It is the six major chakras that correlate with basic states of consciousness...

Susan Shumsky (2003, p. 24) states a similar idea:

> Each chakra in your spinal column is believed to influence or even govern bodily functions near its region of the spine. Because autopsies do not reveal chakras, most people think they are a fancy of fertile imagination. Yet their existence is well documented in the traditions of the far east...

Chakras, as described above, are energy centers along the spine located at major branchings of the human nervous system, beginning at the base of the spinal column and moving upward to the top of the skull, through which pass 3 major energy channels, Sushumna, Ida and Pingala. Chakras are considered to be a point or nexus of biophysical energy or *prana* of the human body. Shumsky states that "prana is the basic component of your subtle body, your energy field, and the entire chakra system...the key to life and source of energy in the universe."

The following seven primary chakras are commonly described:

1. Muladhara (Sanskrit: मूलाधार, Mūlādhāra) Base or Root Chakra (ovaries/prostate)
2. Swadhisthana (Sanskrit: स्वाधिष्ठान, Svādhiṣṭhāna) Sacral Chakra (last bone in spinal cord, the coccyx)
3. Manipura (Sanskrit: मणिपूर, Maṇipūra) Solar Plexus Chakra (navel area)
4. Anahata (Sanskrit: अनाहत, Anāhata) Heart Chakra (heart area)
5. Vishuddha (Sanskrit: विशुद्ध, Viśuddha) Throat Chakra (throat and neck area)
6. Ajna (Sanskrit: आज्ञा, Ājñā) Brow or Third Eye Chakra (pineal gland or third eye)
7. Sahasrara (Sanskrit: सहस्रार, Sahasrāra) Crown Chakra (Top of the head; 'Soft spot' of a newborn)

Chakras

Muladhara   Swadhisthana   Manipura   Anahata   Vishudda   Ajna

Sahasrara

In addition, a number of other chakras are postulated. B.K.S Iyengar states that between the navel and the heart are the Manas (mind) and Surya (sun) chakras, and that at the top of the forehead is the Lalata chakra. The Tibetan tantric tradition has the Fire Wheel between the heart and the throat, the Wind Wheel on the forehead, and below the navel, instead of Swadhisthana and Muladhara, they have 3 chakras; the Secret Place Wheel is located 4 fingers below the navel, the Jewel Wheel is located on the sexual organ, and the very tip of the sexual organ is the very last chakra, where the central channel ends. Other traditions, such as the Bihar school of yoga, add Bindu chakra, which exists at the back of the head, and is where the divine nectar or Amrit is stored, place Lalata chakra in the roof of the mouth, and place Hrit chakra below the heart.

Many traditions posit a number of higher chakras in the head, which from lowest to highest are: golata, talu/talana/lalana, ajna, talata/lalata, manas, soma, sahasrara (and sri inside it.)

Models

The study of the Chakras is a central part of many esoteric traditions, as well as to many different therapies and disciplines. In the east, the theory of chakras is a central part of the Hindu and Buddhist tantra, and they play an important role in attaining deep levels of realisation. Yoga, Pranayama, Acupuncture, shiatsu, tai chi and chi kung focus on balancing the energetic nadis or meridians that are an integral part of the chakra system. Within the West, subtle energy is explored through practices such as aromatherapy, mantras, Reiki, hands-on healing, flower essences, radionics, sound therapy, colour/light therapy, and crystal/gem therapy, to name a few. Several models will be explored in the following sub-headings

Hindu Tantra

In Hinduism, the concept of chakras is part of a complex of ideas related to esoteric anatomy. These ideas occur most often in the class of texts that are called Āgamas or Tantras. This is a large body of scripture, most of which is rejected by the traditionalists. The chakras are described in the tantric texts the *Sat-Cakra-Nirupana*, and the *Padaka-Pancaka*, in which they are described as emanations of consciousness from Brahman, an energy emanating from the spiritual which gradually turns concrete, creating these distinct levels of chakras, and which eventually finds its rest in the Muladhara chakra. They are therefore part of an emanationist theory, like that of the kabbalah in the west, lataif-e-sitta in Sufism or neo-platonism. The energy that was unleashed in creation, called the Kundalini, lies coiled and sleeping at the base of the spine. It is the purpose of the tantric or kundalini forms of yoga to arouse this energy, and cause it to rise back up through the increasingly subtle chakras, until union with God is achieved in the Sahasrara chakra at the crown of the head.

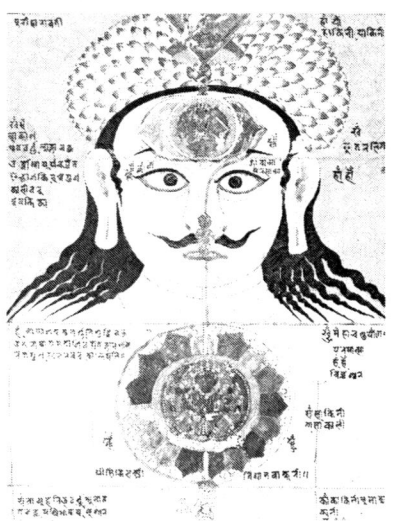

Thousand Petalled Crown Chakra, Two Petalled Brow Chakra, Sixteen Petalled Throat Chakra (Nepal, 17th Century)

There are many variations on these concepts in the Sanskrit source texts. In earlier texts there are various systems of chakras and nadis, with varying connections between them. Various traditional sources list 5, 6, 7, 8 or even 12 chakras. Over time, one system of 6 or 7 chakras along the body's axis became the dominant model, adopted by most schools of yoga. This particular system may have originated in about the 11th century AD, and rapidly became widely popular.

The central role of the chakras in this model is the raising of Kundalini, where it pierces the various centers, causing various levels of realisation and resulting in the obtention of various siddhis or occult powers, until reaching the crown of the head, resulting in union with the Divine. The methods on how to raise kundalini are generally secret, but a number of methods have been published, for example the Bihar school of yoga begin with a number of preparatory practices such as asanas and pranayama to purify the nadis, and then a number of practices and meditations specific to each chakra, and finally the raising of the kundalini through special kriyas, which terminate in the vision of ones causal self

Vajrayana (Buddhist Tantra)

The Tibetan theory of chakras play an important role in all the Highest Yoga Tantras. They play a pivotal role in all Completion stage practices (as opposed to Generation stage practices), where an attempt is made to bring all the subtle winds of the body into the central channel, to realise the clear light of bliss and emptiness, and to attain the 'illusory body' of a divinity .

The Tibetan system states that the central channel begins at the point of the third eye, curves up to the crown of the head, and then goes straight down the body to the tip of the sexual organ. The 2 side channels run parallel to, and without any space in between, the central channel, but they begin at the 2 nostrils, the lunar channel ends in the sexual organ, and the solar channel in the anus. Along the central channel are positioned 10 chakras, of which usually 4 or 5 are expounded as being important. They are located in the following positions:

1. Third eye between the eyebrows
2. The wind wheel on the forehead
3. The crown wheel on the top of the head
4. The throat wheel
5. The fire wheel between the throat and the heart
6. The heart wheel
7. The navel wheel
8. The secret place, 4 fingers below the navel
9. The jewel wheel on the sexual organ, near the end
10. The tip of the sexual organ

The channels run through parallel through them, but at the navel, heart, throat and crown the 2 side channels twist around the central channel. At the navel, throat and crown, there is a 2-fold knot caused by each side channel twisting once around the central channel. At the heart wheel there is a 6-fold knot, where each side channel twists around 3 times. An important part of completion stage practice involves loosening and undoing these knots.

Within the chakras exist the 'subtle drops'. The white drop exists in the crown, the red drop exists in the navel, and at the heart exists the indestructible red and white drop, which leaves the body at the time of death. In addition, each chakra has a number of 'spokes' or 'petals', which branch off into thousands of subtle channels running to every part of the body, and each contains a Sanskrit syllable.

By visualising a specific chakra, the subtle winds (which follow the mind), enter the central channel. The chakra at which they enter is important in order to realise specific practices, for example, meditating on the syllable 'Ah' in the navel chakra is important for the practice of Tummo, or inner fire, the basis of the 6 yogas of Naropa. Meditating on the 'Hum' in the heart chakra is important for realising the Clear Light of bliss and emptiness. Meditating on the throat chakra is important for lucid dreaming and the practices of dream yoga. And meditating on the crown chakra is important for consciousness projection, either to another world, or into another body.

In general, the higher tantras, starting with the Guhyasamaja tantra, are very uniform in their descriptions of the chakras, channels and drops. The Kalachakra tantra has a slightly different system, which also relates the chakras with astrology.

According to contemporary Buddhist teacher Tarthang Tulku, the heart chakra is very important for the feeling of existential fulfilment.[citation needed]

A result of energetic imbalance between chakras is an almost continuous feeling of dissatisfaction. When the heart chakra is agitated, people lose touch with feelings and sensations, and that breeds the sense of dissatisfaction. That leads to looking outside for fulfilment.

When people live in their heads, feelings are secondary, they are interpretations of mental images that are fed back to the individual. When awareness is focused on memories of past experiences and mental verbalisations, the energy flow to the head chakra increases and the energy flow to the heart chakra lessens. Without nurturing feelings of the heart a subtle form of anxiety arises which results in the self reaching out for experience.

When the throat chakra settles and energy is distributed evenly between the head and the heart chakras, one is able to truly contact one's senses and touch real feelings.

Chögyal Namkai Norbu Rinpoche teaches a version of the Six Lokas sadhana which works with the chakra system.[citation needed]

The kye-rim (Tibetan) and dzog-rim (Tibetan) stages work with the 'chakra' (Tibetan: *khorlo*). [citation needed]

Bön

Chakras, as pranic centers of the body, according to the Himalayan Bönpo tradition, influence the quality of experience, because movement of prana can not be separated from experience. Each of the six major chakras are linked to experiential qualities of one of the six realms of existence.

A modern teacher, Tenzin Wangyal Rinpoche uses a computer analogy: main chakras are like hard drives. Each hard drive has many files. One of the files is always open in each of the chakras, no matter how "closed" that particular chakra may be. What is displayed by the file shapes experience.

The tsa lung practices such as those embodied in Trul Khor lineages open channels so *lung* (*Lung* is a Tibetan term cognate with prana or qi) may move without obstruction. Yoga opens chakras and evokes positive qualities associated with a particular chakra. In the hard drive analogy, the screen is cleared and a file is called up that contains positive, supportive qualities. A seed syllable (Sanskrit bija) is used both as a password that evokes the positive quality and the armour that sustains the quality.

Tantric practice is said to eventually transform all experience into bliss. The practice aims to liberate from negative conditioning and leads to control over perception and cognition.

Tenzin Wangyal Rinpoche teaches a version of the Six Lokas sadhana which works with the chakra system.

Western derivative models and interpretations

In the Western hemisphere, a concept similar to that of prana can be traced back as far as the 18th century's Franz Anton Mesmer that used 'animal magnetism' to cure disease, however it is only in 1927 that the shakta theory of 7 main chakras that has become most popular in the Western hemisphere was introduced, largely through the translation of two Indian texts, the *Sat-Cakra-Nirupana*, and the *Padaka-Pancaka*, by Sir John Woodroffe, alias Arthur Avalon, in a book titled *The Serpent Power*. This book is extremely detailed and complex, and later the ideas were developed into what is the predominant Western view of the Chakras by C. W. Leadbeater in his book *The Chakras*. Many of Leadbeater's views that directed his understanding of chakras were influenced by previous theosophist authors and in particular Johann Georg Gichtel, a disciple of Jakob Böhme, and his book *Theosophia Practica (1696)* in which Gitchtel directly refer to inner *force centers*, a concept reminiscent of that of chakras..

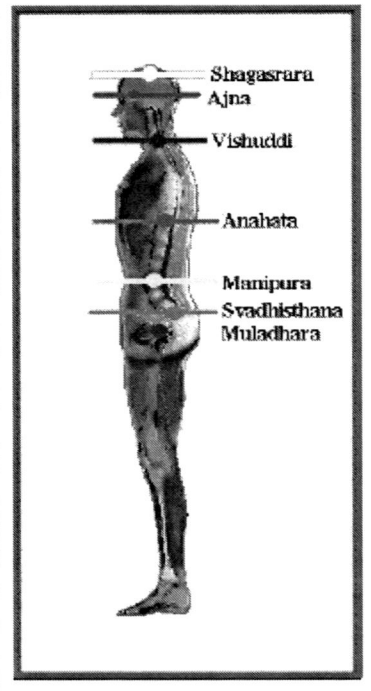

Due to the similarities between the Chinese and Indian philosophies, the notion of chakras was quickly amalgamated to Chinese practices such as acupuncture and belief in ki. The confluence of these two divergent healing traditions and the common practitioners' own inventiveness have led to an ever-changing and expanding array of concepts in the Western world. According to medical intuitive and author, Caroline Myss, who described chakras in her work *Anatomy of the Spirit* (1996), "Every thought and experience you've ever had in your life gets filtered through these chakra databases. Each event is recorded into your cells...", in effect your biography becomes your biology.

The chakras are described as being aligned in an ascending column from the base of the spine to the top of the head. In New Age practices, each chakra is often associated with a certain colour. In various traditions chakras are associated with multiple physiological functions, an aspect of consciousness, a classical element, and other distinguishing characteristics. They are visualized as lotuses/flowers with a different number of petals in every chakra.

The chakras are thought to vitalise the physical body and to be associated with interactions of a physical, emotional and mental nature. They are considered loci of life energy or prana, also called shakti, qi (Chinese; *ki* in Japanese), koach-ha-guf (Hebrew), bios (Greek) & aether (Greek, English), which is thought to flow among them along pathways called nadis. The function of the chakras is to spin and draw in this energy to keep the spiritual, mental, emotional and physical health of the body in balance, and are said by some to reflect how the unified consciousness of humanity (the immortal human being or the soul), is divided to manage different aspects of earthly life (body/instinct/vital energy/deeper emotions/communication/having an overview of life/contact to God). The chakras are placed at differing levels of spiritual subtlety, with Sahasrara at the top being concerned with pure consciousness, and Muladhara at the bottom being concerned with matter, which is seen simply as crudified consciousness.

Rudolf Steiner (one-time Theosophist, and founder of Anthroposophy) says much about the Chakras that is unusual, especially that the chakra system is dynamic and evolving and is very different for modern people than it was in ancient times, and will in turn be radically different in future times. In contrast to the traditional eastern teachings, Steiner describes a sequence of development from the top down rather than the bottom up. This is the so called 'Christos Path' which has not always been available to humanity. [This is also revealed by Swami Sivananda in his book on Japa Yoga, Himalaya Press 1978. In which the Swami states that a yogi that practices Japa with only the Om and is successful at Mahasamyama {oneness with the object...in this case a Word being meditated on} becomes a direct disciple of that, the OM, the most Holy of all words/syllables { the same as the word of creation as recognized by the Torah, although this is not professed or quite possibly not even recognized by those of secular authority in either Hebraism or Christianity} thus the yogi achieving this feat needs no Guru or Sat-guru* to achieve any Spiritual goal {*Archetype / Ascended Master i.e. A Krishna, a Rama, a Jesus, a Nanak a Buddha..et al} and Swami Sivananda mentions that this yogi has a path that is, in all recognizable ways and manners, reverse that of other Yogis or Spiritual aspirants and their paths and those include all Christian ascetics, in that this spiritual aspirant then works through the chakras, mastering them from the Crown down. Where-as every other well known path of all major religions start by trying to master the chakras starting with the 'Svadhisthana Chakra' {Sex} These Yogis aren't expected to renunciate sex or certain foods and by virtue of this they do not need to remove themselves from the world of temptations become monks/recluses. They stay in the world of men and live what appears to be a normal life that is relative to whatever local custom{s} that may be. Trevor Ravenscroft also mentions this spiritual goal and achievement in His book, "The Cup Of Destiny", and says it was known and the most highly regarded and desired practice and achievement for the Templar Knights of old.] He also seems to ignore the Thousand Petalled chakra at the crown of the head and instead cryptically mentions an Eight Petalled chakra located between the Ten Petalled and the Six Petalled ones. In his book *How to Know Higher Worlds* Steiner gives clear instructions on how to develop the chakras safely into maturity. These are more like life disciplines than exercises and can take considerable time. He warns that while quicker methods exist, they can be dangerous to one's health, character, or sanity.[*citation needed*]

New Age writers, such as Anodea Judith in her book *Wheels of Life*, have written about the chakras in great detail, including the reasons for their appearance and functions.

Another unique interpretation of the seven chakras is presented by writer and artist Zachary Selig. In the book *Kundalini Awakening, a Gentle Guide to Chakra Activation and Spiritual Growth,* he presents a unique codex titled "Relaxatia", a solar Kundalini paradigm that is a codex of the human chakra system and the solar light spectrum, designed to activate Kundalini through his colour-coded chakra paintings.

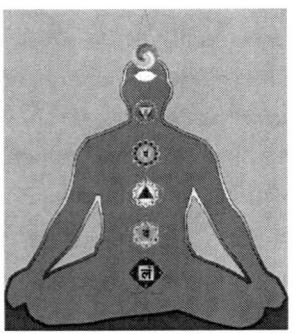

Yoga Asana pose and chakras

Additionally, some chakra system models describe one or more Transpersonal chakras above the crown chakra, and an Earth star chakra below the feet. There are also held to be many minor chakras, for example between the major chakras. Chakras are also used in neurolinguistic programming to connect NLP logical levels with spiritual goals on the crown, intellectual on the forehead and so on.

Endocrine system

The primary importance and level of existence of chakras is posited to be in the psyche. However, there are those who believe that chakras have a physical manifestation as well. The author Gary Osborn, for instance, has described the chakras as metaphysical counterparts to the endocrine glands, while Anodea Judith noted a marked similarity between the positions of the two and the roles described for each. Stephen Sturgess also links the lower six chakras to specific nerve plexuses along the spinal cord as well as glands. C.W. Leadbeater associated the Anja chakra with the pineal gland, which is a part of the endocrine system. Edgar Cayce said that the 7 churches of the Book of Revelation are endocrine glands.

The Spectrum of Light

A recent development in Western practices dating back to the 1940s is to associate each one of the seven chakras to a given colour and a corresponding crystal. For example, the chakra in the forehead is associated with the colour purple, so to cure a headache you would apply a purple stone to the forehead. This idea has proven highly popular and has been integrated by all but a few practitioners.

Mercier introduces the relation of colour energy to the science of the light spectrum;

> "As humans, we exist within the 49th Octave of Vibration of the electromagnetic light spectrum. Below this range are barely visible radiant heat, then invisible infrared, television and radiowaves, sound and brain waves; above it is barely visible ultraviolet, then the invisible frequencies of chemicals and perfumes, followed by x-rays, gamma rays, radium rays and unknown cosmic rays.

Understanding existence and physical form as an interpretation of light energy through the physical eyes will open up greater potential to explore the energetic boundaries of color, form and light that are perceived as immediate reality. Indian Yogic teachings assign to the seven major chakras specific qualities, such as color of influence (from the 7 rays of spectrum light), elements (such as earth, air, water & ether), body sense (such as touch, taste, and smell), and relation to an endocrine gland.

Description of the chakras

Tantric chakras
Sahasrara
Ajna
Vishuddha
Anahata
Manipura
Swadhisthana
Muladhara
Bindu

7 chakras in particular are described in the Shakta Tantra tradition that was brought over to the West. Below is a description of each of them, with Eastern and Western associations.

Sahasrara: The Crown Chakra

Sahasrara, which means 100 petalled lotus, is generally considered to be the chakra of pure consciousness, within which there is neither object nor subject. When the female kundalini Shakti energy rises to this point, it unites with the male Shiva energy, and a state of liberating samadhi is attained. Symbolized by a lotus with one thousand multi-coloured petals, it is located either at the crown of the head, or above the crown of the head. Sahasrara is represented by the colour white and it involves such issues as inner wisdom and the death of the body. Its role may be envisioned somewhat similarly to that of the pituitary gland, which secretes hormones to communicate to the rest of the endocrine system and also connects to the central nervous system via the hypothalamus. According to author Gary Osborn, the thalamus is thought to have a key role in the physical basis of consciousness and is the 'Bridal Chamber' mentioned in the Gnostic scriptures. Sahasrara's inner aspect deals with the release of karma, physical action with meditation, mental action with universal consciousness and unity, and emotional action with "beingness".

In Tibetan buddhism, the point at the crown of the head is represented by a white circle, with 32 downward pointing petals. It is of primary importance in the performance of phowa, or consciousness projection after death, in order to obtain rebirth in a Pure Land. Within this chakra is contained the White drop, or Bodhicitta, which is the essence of masculine energy.

Ajna: The Brow Chakra

Ajna is symbolised by a lotus with two petals, and corresponds to the colors violet, indigo or deep blue. It is at this point that the 2 side nadis Ida and Pingala are said to terminate and merge with the central channel Sushumna, signifying the end of duality. The seed syllable for this chakra is the syllable OM, and the presiding deity is Ardhanarishvara, who is a half male, half female Shiva/Shakti. The Shakti goddess of Ajna is called Hakini. Ajna (along with Bindu), is known as the third eye chakra and is linked to the pineal gland which may inform a model of its envisioning. The pineal gland is a light sensitive gland that produces the hormone melatonin which regulates sleep and waking up. Ajna's key issues involve balancing the higher & lower selves and trusting inner guidance. Ajna's inner aspect relates to the access of intuition. Mentally, Ajna deals with visual consciousness. Emotionally, Ajna deals with clarity on an intuitive level. (Note: some opine that the pineal and pituitary glands should be exchanged in their relationship to the Crown and Brow chakras, based on the description in Arthur Avalon's book on kundalini called *Serpent Power* or empirical research.)

In Tibetan Buddhism, this point is actually the end of the central channel, since the central channel rises up from the sexual organ to the crown of the head, and then curves over the head and down to the third eye. While the central channel finishes here, the two side channels continue down to the 2 nostrils.

Vishuddha: The Throat Chakra

Vishuddha (also Vishuddhi) is depicted as a silver crescent within a white circle, with 16 light or pale blue, or turquoise petals. The seed mantra is Ham, and the residing deity is Panchavaktra shiva, with 5 heads and 4 arms, and the Shakti is Shakini. Vishuddha may be understood as relating to communication and growth through expression. This chakra is paralleled to the thyroid, a gland that is also in the throat and which produces thyroid hormone, responsible for growth and maturation. Physically, Vishuddha governs communication, emotionally it governs independence, mentally it governs fluent thought, and spiritually, it governs a sense of security. In Tibetan buddhism, this chakra is red, with 16 upward pointing petals. It plays an important role in Dream Yoga, the art of lucid dreaming.

Anahata: The Heart Chakra

Anahata, or Anahata-puri, or padma-sundara is symbolised by a circular flower with twelve vermillion, or green petals. (See also heartmind). Within it is a yantra of 2 intersecting triangles, forming a star of David, symbolising a union of the male and female. The seed mantra is Yam, the presiding deity is Ishana Rudra Shiva, and the Shakti is Kakini.

Anahata is related to the thymus, located in the chest. The thymus is an element of the immune system as well as being part of the endocrine system. It is the site of maturation of the T cells responsible for fending off disease and may be adversely affected by stress. . Anahata is related to the colours green or pink. Key issues involving Anahata involve complex emotions, compassion, tenderness, unconditional love, equilibrium, rejection and well-being. Physically Anahata governs circulation, emotionally it governs unconditional love for the self and others, mentally it governs passion, and spiritually it governs devotion.

In Tibetan buddhism, this centre is extremely important, as being the home of the indestructible red/white drop, which carries our consciousness to our next lives. It is described as being white, circular, with 8 downward pointing petals, and the seed syllable Hum inside. During mantra recitation in the lower tantras, a flame is imagined inside of the heart, from which the mantra rings out. Within the higher tantras, this chakra is very important for realising the Clear Light.

Manipura: The Solar Plexus Chakra

Manipura or manipuraka is symbolised by a downward pointing triangle with ten petals. The seed syllable is Ram, and the presiding deity is Braddha Rudra, with Lakini as the Shakti.

Manipura is related to the metabolic and digestive systems. Manipura is believed to correspond to Islets of Langerhans, which are groups of cells in the pancreas, as well as the outer adrenal glands and the adrenal cortex. These play a valuable role in digestion, the conversion of food matter into energy for the body. The colour that corresponds to Manipura is yellow. Key issues governed by Manipura are issues of personal power, fear, anxiety, opinion-formation, introversion, and transition from simple or base emotions to complex. Physically, Manipura governs digestion, mentally it governs personal power, emotionally it governs expansiveness, and spiritually, all matters of growth.

In Tibetan buddhism, this wheel is represented as a triangle with 64 upward pointing petals. It is the home of the Red drop, or red bodhicitta, which is the essence of feminine energy (as opposed to the Shakta system, where the kundalini energy resides in Muladhara). It contains the seed syllable short-Ah, which is of primary importance in the Tummo inner fire meditation, which is the system by which the energy of the red drop is raised to the white drop in the crown.

Svadhisthana: The Sacral Chakra

Swadhisthana, Svadisthana or adhishthana is symbolized by a white lotus within which is a crescent moon, with six vermillion, or orange petals. The seed mantra is Vam, and the presiding deity is either Vishnu, with the Shakti being Rakini (or Chakini). The animal associated is the crocodile of Varuna. The Sacral Chakra is located in the sacrum (hence the name) and is considered to correspond to the testes or the ovaries that produce the various sex hormones involved in the reproductive cycle. Svadisthana is also considered to be related to, more generally, the genitourinary system and the adrenals. The key issues involving Svadisthana are relationships, violence, addictions, basic emotional needs, and pleasure. Physically, Svadisthana governs reproduction, mentally it governs creativity, emotionally it governs joy, and spiritually it governs enthusiasm.

In Tibetan buddhism, this is known as the Secret Place wheel. Below this point the Shakta tantra and Vajrayana systems diverge somewhat.

Muladhara: The Base Chakra

Muladhara or root chakra is represented as a yellow square, with 4 red petals. The seed syllable is Lam, the deity is Brahma, and the Shakti is Dakini. The associated animal is the elephant Ganesha. This chakra is where the 3 channels are merged, then separate and begin their upward movement. Inside of this chakra is wrapped up the goddess kundalini three times around a black lingam. It is the seat of the red bindu, the female drop (which in Tibetan vajrayana is located at the navel chakra).

is related to instinct, security, survival and also to basic human potentiality. This center is located in the perineum, which is the region between the genital and the anus. Although no endocrine organ is placed here, it is said to relate to the gonads and the adrenal medulla, responsible for the fight-or-flight response when survival is under threat. There is a muscle located in this region that controls ejaculation in the sexual act of the human male. A parallel is charted between the sperm cell and the ovum where the genetic code lies coiled and the kundalini. Muladhara is symbolized by a lotus with four petals and the colour red. Key issues involve sexuality, lust and obsession. Physically, Muladhara governs sexuality, mentally it governs stability, emotionally it governs sensuality, and spiritually it governs a sense of security.

There is no chakra that exists in this position within Tibetan buddhism. Instead, below the secret place wheel, there are 2 other wheels, the jewel wheel, which is located in the middle of the sex organ, and the wheel located at the tip of the sex organ. These wheels are extremely important for the generation of great bliss, and are involved with tantric consort practices.

The Minor Chakras

In addition to the 7 major chakras, there are a number of other chakras which have importance within different systems. For example, Woodroffe describes 7 head chakras (including Ajna and Sahasrara) in his other Indian text sources. Lowest to highest they are: Talu/Talana/Lalana, Ajna, Manas, Soma, Brahmarandra, Sri (inside Sahasrara), Sahasrara. In addition, the chakra Hrit known as the wish-fulfilling tree is often included below the heart, which may be the same as a chakra known as Surya located at the solar plexus. Some models also have a series of 7 lower chakras below muladhara that go down the legs.

Hrit chakra or Surya chakra

This chakra is a minor chakra located just below the heart at the solar plexus, and is known as the wish-fulfilling tree. Here, the ability to determine your destiny becomes a reality. It is also known as the Surya chakra . It supports the actions of Manipura chakra by providing it with the element of heat, and is responsible for absorbing energy from the sun.

In Tibetan buddhism, a similar chakra called the Fire Wheel is included in the scheme, but this is located above the heart and below the throat.

Lalana/Talumula

A chakra known as Lalana is situated in one of two places, either in the roof of the mouth, between Visuddhi and Ajna, or on the forehead, above Ajna. The Lalana chakra on the roof of the mouth is related to Bindu and Vishuddhi. When the nectar amrit trickles down from Bindu, it is stored in lalana. This nectar can fall down to Manipura and be burned up, causing gradual degeneration, or through certain practices it can be passed to Visuddhi and purified, becoming a nectar of immortality.

Manas

A chakra known as Manas (mind) is located either between the navel and the heart, close to Surya, or is located above Ajna on the forehead. The version on the forehead has 6 petals, connected to the 5 sense objects plus the mind. In Tibetan buddhism, the chakra located on the forehead is called the Wind wheel, and has 6 spokes.

Bindu Visarga/Indu/Chandra

Bindu visarga, is located either at the top back of the head, where some Brahmins leave a tuft of hair growing, or in the middle forehead. It is symbolised by a crescent moon. This chakra secretes an ambrosial fluid, amrit, and is the seat of the white bindu (compare with the white bodhicitta drop in the crown chakra in the Vajrayana system).

Brahmarandra/Nirvana

In some systems, Sahasrara is the chakra that is on the crown of the head. However, other systems, such as that expounded by Shri Aurobindo, state that the real Sahasrara is located some way above the top of the head, and that the crown chakra is in fact Brahmarandra, a sort of secondary Sahasrara with 100 white petals.

Shri/Guru

This is a minor chakra located slightly above the top of the head. It is an upward facing 12 petalled lotus, and it is associated with the Guru, that higher force that guides us through our spiritual journey.

Lower Chakras

There are said to be a series of 7 chakras below muladhara going down the leg, corresponding the base animal instincts, and to the Hindu underworld patala. They are called atala, vitala, sutala, talatala, rasatala, mahatala and patala.

Atala

This chakra is located in the hips, it governs fear and lust.

Vitala

Located in the thighs, it governs anger and resentment.

Sutala

Located in the knees, it governs jealousy.

Talatala

Translated as 'under the bottom level', it is located in the calves, and it is a state of prolonged confusion and instinctive wilfulness.

Rasatala

Located in the ankles, it is the centre of selfishness and pure animal nature.

Mahatala

Located in the feet, this is the dark realm 'without conscience', and inner blindness.

Patala

Located in the soles of the feet, this is the realm of malice, murder, torture and hatred, and in Hindu mythology it borders on the realm of Naraka, or Hell.

Others

There are said to be 21 minor chakras which are reflected points of the major chakras. These 21 are further grouped into 10 bilateral minor chakras that correspond to the foot, hand, knee, elbow, groin, clavicular, navel, shoulder and ear. The spleen may also be classified as a minor chakra by some authorities despite not having an associated coupled minor chakra.

Comparisons with other Esoteric Traditions

A number of other mystical traditions talk about subtle energies that flow through the body, and identify specific parts of the body as being subtle centres. There are many similarities between systems, however, none of these traditions developed in isolation; the Indian mystical traditions had contact with the Chinese and Islamic mystical traditions, and they may have mutually influenced one another. Similarly, the Jewish and Islamic mystical traditions shared a great deal in common, especially during the Islamic occupation of Spain, and Jewish mysticism in particular had influence over Christian mysticism.

Qigong, the Dantian

Qigong also relies on a similar model of the human body as an energy system, except that it involves the circulation of qi (ki, chi) energy.. The Qi energy, equivalent to the Hindu Prana, flows through the energy channels called meridians, equivalent to the nadis, but 2 other energies are also important, Jing, the sexual energy, and Shen, or spirit energy.

In the principle circuit of qi, called the Microcosmic orbit, energy rises up a main meridian along the spine, but also comes back down the front torso. Throughout its cycle it enters various dantians (elixir fields) which act as furnaces, where the types of energy in the body (jing, qi and shen) are progressively refined . These Dantians play a very similar role to that of chakras. The number of Dantians varies depending on the system; the navel dantian is the most well-known (it is called the Hara in Japan), but there is usually a Dantian located at the heart and between the eyebrows. The lower dantian at or below the navel transforms sexual essence, or jing, into qi energy. The middle dantian in the middle of the chest transforms qi energy into shen, or spirit, and the higher dantian at the level of the forehead (or at the top of the head), transforms Shen into wuji, infinite space of void .

In Japan, the word qi is written ki, and is related to the practice of Reiki, and plays an important role in Japanese martial arts such as Aikido.

Sufism, the Lataif

Many Sufi orders make use of Lata'if, subtle centres in the body which are between 4 or 7 in number, and relate to ever more subtle levels of intimacy with Allah. But although some Lataif correspond in position to the chakras, there are also some big differences in position and meaning.

One 6 lata'if system positions the Nafs, or lower self, below the navel, the Qalb, or heart, in the left of the chest, the Ruh, or spirit, to the right of the chest, the Sirr, or secret, in the solar plexus, the Khafi, or latent subtlety, in the position of the third eye, and the Akhfa, or most arcane, at the top of the head. They are frequently associated with a colour, as well as a particular prophet.

Unlike the Indian and Chinese system, the emphasis is not upon these subtle centres performing a kind of inner alchemy upon the energies of the body, such as kundalini awakening, and they are not considered like organs for the subtle body; instead, they represent more abstract, philosophical concepts, representing ever greater degrees of closeness to Allah.

Christianity, Hesychasm

A completely separate contemplative movement within the Eastern Orthodox church is Hesychasm, a form of Christian meditation. Comparisons have been made between the Hesychastic centres of prayer and the position of the chakras . Particular emphasis is placed upon the heart area. However, there is no talk about these centres as having any sort of metaphysical existence. Far more than in any of the cases discussed above, the centres are simply places to focus the concentration during prayer.

Other mystical traditions exist within Christianity. The Renaissance saw the birth of 'Christian Kabbalah', which had its roots in Jewish kabbalah.

Etymology

Bhattacharyya's review of Tantric history says that the word *chakra* is used to mean several different things in the Sanskrit sources:

1. "Circle", used in a variety of senses, symbolizing endless rotation of shakti.
2. A circle of people. In rituals there are different *cakra-sādhanā* in which adherents assemble and perform rites. According to the *Niruttaratantra*, chakras in the sense of assemblies are of 5 types.
3. The term chakra also is used to denote yantras or mystic diagrams, variously known as *trikoṇa-cakra, aṣṭakoṇa-cakra*, etc.
4. Different "nerve plexus within the body".

In Buddhist literature the Sanskrit term *cakra* (Pali *cakka*) is used in a different sense of "circle", referring to a Buddhist conception of the 4 circles or states of existence in which gods or men may find themselves.

The linguist Jorma Koivulehto wrote (2001) of the annual Finnish *Kekri* celebration having loaned the word from early Indo-Aryan. Indo-European cognates include Greek *kuklos*, Lithuanian *kaklas*,

Tocharian B *kokale* and English "wheel".

Cognates of "chakra" still exist in modern Asian languages as well. In Malay, "cakera" means "disc", e.g. "cakera padat" = "compact disc".

See also

- Hindu tantra
- Subpersonal chakras
- Third eye
- Transpersonal chakras
- Endocrine system

References

- BelindaGrace (2007). *You are Clairvoyant - Developing the secret skill we all have* [1]. Rockpool Publishing.
- Apte, Vaman Shivram (1965). *The Practical Sanskrit Dictionary* (fourth revised & enlarged ed.). Delhi: Motilal Banarsidass Publishers. ISBN 81-208-0567-4.
- Bhattacharyya, N. N. (1999). *History of the Tantric Religion* (Second Revised ed.). New Delhi: Manohar. pp. 174. ISBN 81-7304-025-7.
- Bucknell, Roderick; Stuart-Fox, Martin (1986). *The Twilight Language: Explorations in Buddhist Meditation and Symbolism*. London: Curzon Press. ISBN 0-312-82540-4.
- Edgerton, Franklin (2004) [1953]. *Buddhist Hybrid Sanskrit Grammar and Dictionary* (Reprint ed.). Delhi: Motilal Banarsidass Publishers. ISBN 81-208-0999-8. (Two volumes)
- Flood, Gavin (1996). *An Introduction to Hinduism*. Cambridge: Cambridge University Press. ISBN 0-521-43878-0.
- Chia, Mantak; Chia, Maneewan (1993). *Awaken Healing Light of the Tao*. Healing Tao Books.
- Monier-Williams, Monier. *A Sanskrit-English Dictionary*. Delhi: Motilal Banarsidass Publishers.
- Prabhananda, S. (2000). *Studies on the Tantras* (Second reprint ed.). Calcutta: The Ramakrishna Mission Institute of Culture. ISBN 81-85843-36-8.
- Rinpoche, Tenzin Wangyal (2002). *Healing with Form, Energy, and Light*. Ithaca, New York: Snow Lion Publications. ISBN 1559391766.
- Saraswati, MD, Swami Sivananda (1953 - 2001). *Kundalini Yoga*. Tehri-Garhwal, India: Divine Life Society. foldout chart. ISBN 81-7052-052-5.
- Tulku, Tarthang (2007). *Tibetan Relaxation. The illustrated guide to Kum Nye massage and movement - A yoga from the Tibetan tradition*. London: Dunkan Baird Publishers. ISBN 978-1-84483-404-4.
- Woodroffe, John (1919 - 1964). *The Serpent Power*. Madras, India: Ganesh & Co.. ISBN 0-486-23058-9.

Further reading

Traditional secondary sources and commentary

- Banerji, S. C. *Tantra in Bengal*. Second Revised and Enlarged Edition. (Manohar: Delhi, 1992) ISBN 81-85425-63-9
- Saraswati, Swami Sivananda, MD (1953 - 2001). *Kundalini Yoga*. Tehri-Garhwal, India: Divine Life Society. ISBN 81-7052-052-5.
- Shyam Sundar Goswami, *Layayoga: The Definitive Guide to the Chakras and Kundalini*, Routledge & Kegan Paul, 1980.

Western and interpretive literature

- Leadbeater, C.W. *The Chakras* Wheaton, Illinois, U.S.A.:1926—Theosophical Publishing House—Picture of the Chakras on plates facing page 17 as claimed to have been observed by Leadbeater with his *third eye* Full text of the book "The Chakras" by C.W. Leadbeater with colour illustrations of the chakras: [2]
- Sharp, Dr. Michael (2005). *Dossier of the Ascension: A Practical Guide to Chakra Activation and Kundalini Awakening* [3] (1st ed.). Avatar Publications. ISBN 0973537930.
- Guru Dharam S Khalsa and Darryl OKeeffe. *The Kundalini Yoga Experience* New York, NY U.S.A.:2002, Fireside, Simon & Schuster, Inc. Copyright by Baia Books Limited. Kriyans and meditations copyright Yogi Bhajan, All Rights reserved.
- Judith, Anodea (1996). *Eastern Body Western Mind: Psychology And The Chakra System As A Path To The Self*. Berkeley, California, USA: Celestial Arts Publishing. ISBN 0-89087-815-3
- Dahlheimer, Dr. Volker (2006). *Kundalini Shakti: Explanation of the Seven Chakras* [4] (Video clip with words and explanative grafics ed.). 5th Level Publications.

External links

- Sites related to chakra [5] at the Open Directory Project

Article Sources and Contributors

Abbey of Thelema *Source*: http://en.wikipedia.org/?oldid=389800852 *Contributors*: 1 anonymous edits

Abramelin oil *Source*: http://en.wikipedia.org/?oldid=378234586 *Contributors*: R'n'B

Adept *Source*: http://en.wikipedia.org/?oldid=374782240 *Contributors*: Peccavimus

Akashic records *Source*: http://en.wikipedia.org/?oldid=390636915 *Contributors*: 1 anonymous edits

Alchemy *Source*: http://en.wikipedia.org/?oldid=390488523 *Contributors*: Ian.thomson

Ascended master *Source*: http://en.wikipedia.org/?oldid=368086899 *Contributors*: TheRingess

Astral projection *Source*: http://en.wikipedia.org/?oldid=389354593 *Contributors*: Fæ

Astrology *Source*: http://en.wikipedia.org/?oldid=390675879 *Contributors*: Crusio

Automatic writing *Source*: http://en.wikipedia.org/?oldid=385287776 *Contributors*: Jess

Banishing *Source*: http://en.wikipedia.org/?oldid=367764668 *Contributors*: Kumioko

Bibliomancy *Source*: http://en.wikipedia.org/?oldid=384610209 *Contributors*: 1 anonymous edits

Biosophy *Source*: http://en.wikipedia.org/?oldid=390008083 *Contributors*:

Black magic *Source*: http://en.wikipedia.org/?oldid=390255920 *Contributors*:

Subtle body *Source*: http://en.wikipedia.org/?oldid=389440894 *Contributors*: ENeville

Candomblé *Source*: http://en.wikipedia.org/?oldid=390617399 *Contributors*: 1 anonymous edits

Cartomancy *Source*: http://en.wikipedia.org/?oldid=379566878 *Contributors*: 1 anonymous edits

Clairvoyance *Source*: http://en.wikipedia.org/?oldid=389855445 *Contributors*: Steve3849

Collective unconscious *Source*: http://en.wikipedia.org/?oldid=388924117 *Contributors*: Clocke

Coven *Source*: http://en.wikipedia.org/?oldid=389960350 *Contributors*: Jpb1301

Charmstone *Source*: http://en.wikipedia.org/?oldid=376122079 *Contributors*: 1 anonymous edits

Chakra *Source*: http://en.wikipedia.org/?oldid=390582269 *Contributors*: 1 anonymous edits

Image Sources, Licenses and Contributors

Image:William Fettes Douglas - The Alchemist.jpg *Source*: http://bibliocm.bibliolabs.com/mwAnon/index.php?title=File:William_Fettes_Douglas_-_The_Alchemist.jpg *License*: unknown *Contributors*: AndreasPraefcke, Herrick, Hollyl, Mattes, Plindenbaum, Thuresson, Wst

File:Raimundus Lullus alchemic page.jpg *Source*: http://bibliocm.bibliolabs.com/mwAnon/index.php?title=File:Raimundus_Lullus_alchemic_page.jpg *License*: unknown *Contributors*: Ramon Llull

Image:GoldFlwr3.gif *Source*: http://bibliocm.bibliolabs.com/mwAnon/index.php?title=File:GoldFlwr3.gif *License*: unknown *Contributors*: Richard Wilhelm (trans)

Image:SekienIkiryo.jpg *Source*: http://bibliocm.bibliolabs.com/mwAnon/index.php?title=File:SekienIkiryo.jpg *License*: Public Domain *Contributors*: Wikipedia:Toriyama SekienToriyama Sekien (Wikipedia:ja:鳥山石燕鳥山石燕, Japanese, *1712, †1788)

Image:Astrologyproject.svg *Source*: http://bibliocm.bibliolabs.com/mwAnon/index.php?title=File:Astrologyproject.svg *License*: GNU Free Documentation License *Contributors*: User Chris Brennan on en.wikipedia

Image:HermesTrismegistusCauc.jpg *Source*: http://bibliocm.bibliolabs.com/mwAnon/index.php?title=File:HermesTrismegistusCauc.jpg *License*: Public Domain *Contributors*: user:Tomisti

Image:zodiac woodcut.png *Source*: http://bibliocm.bibliolabs.com/mwAnon/index.php?title=File:Zodiac_woodcut.png *License*: Public Domain *Contributors*: Juiced lemon, Micheletb, Mogelzahn, Warburg, 1 anonymous edits

Image:12 houses of heaven.jpg *Source*: http://bibliocm.bibliolabs.com/mwAnon/index.php?title=File:12_houses_of_heaven.jpg *License*: unknown *Contributors*: User:Micheletb

Image:Anatomical Man.jpg *Source*: http://bibliocm.bibliolabs.com/mwAnon/index.php?title=File:Anatomical_Man.jpg *License*: Public Domain *Contributors*: Anne97432, Berrucomons, Dbenbenn, Hekerui, Hystrix, Leinad-Z, Mattes, Paris 16, Petrusbarbygere, Ranveig, Shizhao, The Evil IP address, W!B:, Wst, Wutsje, [3], [5] anonymous edits

Image:Universum.jpg *Source*: http://bibliocm.bibliolabs.com/mwAnon/index.php?title=File:Universum.jpg *License*: Attribution *Contributors*: Heikenwaelder Hugo, Austria, Email : heikenwaelder@aon.at, www.heikenwaelder.at

Image:Marseffect.svg *Source*: http://bibliocm.bibliolabs.com/mwAnon/index.php?title=File:Marseffect.svg *License*: GNU Free Documentation License *Contributors*: User w:User:Chris BrennanChris Brennan on English Wikipedia

Image:Cellarius ptolemaic system.jpg *Source*: http://bibliocm.bibliolabs.com/mwAnon/index.php?title=File:Cellarius_ptolemaic_system.jpg *License*: Public Domain *Contributors*: Loon, J. van (Johannes), ca. 1611–1686.

Image:God the Geometer.jpg *Source*: http://bibliocm.bibliolabs.com/mwAnon/index.php?title=File:God_the_Geometer.jpg *License*: unknown *Contributors*: Dsmdgold, Gryffindor, Leinad-Z, Mdd, Petropoxy (Lithoderm Proxy), Ragesoss, Shakko, THEN WHO WAS PHONE?, 3 anonymous edits

Image:Sapta Chakra, 1899.jpg *Source*: http://bibliocm.bibliolabs.com/mwAnon/index.php?title=File:Sapta_Chakra,_1899.jpg *License*: Public Domain *Contributors*: Abhishekjoshi, Davin7, Quibik, Redtigerxyz, Roland zh, TheMandarin

Image:Acupuncture chart 300px.jpg *Source*: http://bibliocm.bibliolabs.com/mwAnon/index.php?title=File:Acupuncture_chart_300px.jpg *License*: unknown *Contributors*: Fulcanelli, Jann, Mathieu.clabaut, WolfgangMichel, Xhienne, 1 anonymous edits

Image:Cosmicman.jpg *Source*: http://bibliocm.bibliolabs.com/mwAnon/index.php?title=File:Cosmicman.jpg *License*: Public Domain *Contributors*: Ixitixel, Till.niermann

Image:Casa branca engenho velho.jpg *Source*: http://bibliocm.bibliolabs.com/mwAnon/index.php?title=File:Casa_branca_engenho_velho.jpg *License*: Public Domain *Contributors*: Jurema Oliveira, 1 anonymous edits

Image:Ile opo afonja.jpg *Source*: http://bibliocm.bibliolabs.com/mwAnon/index.php?title=File:Ile_opo_afonja.jpg *License*: Public Domain *Contributors*: Gildemax, Jurema Oliveira

Image:Michail Alexandrowitsch Wrubel 001.jpg *Source*: http://bibliocm.bibliolabs.com/mwAnon/index.php?title=File:Michail_Alexandrowitsch_Wrubel_001.jpg *License*: Public Domain *Contributors*: AndreasPraefcke, Emijrp, Olivier2, Shakko, Wst

file:Ganzfeld.jpg *Source*: http://bibliocm.bibliolabs.com/mwAnon/index.php?title=File:Ganzfeld.jpg *License*: Public Domain *Contributors*: Original uploader was Nealparr at en.wikipedia

File:Freud Sofa.JPG *Source*: http://bibliocm.bibliolabs.com/mwAnon/index.php?title=File:Freud_Sofa.JPG *License*: GNU Free Documentation License *Contributors*: Created by Konstantin Binder

Image:Quartz Crystal.jpg *Source*: http://bibliocm.bibliolabs.com/mwAnon/index.php?title=File:Quartz_Crystal.jpg *License*: Public Domain *Contributors*: USGS

File:Yogin with six chakras, India, Punjab Hills, Kangra, late 18th century.jpg *Source*: http://bibliocm.bibliolabs.com/mwAnon/index.php?title=File:Yogin_with_six_chakras,_India,_Punjab_Hills,_Kangra,_late_18th_century.jpg *License*: Public Domain *Contributors*: Unknown. Original uploader was Redtigerxyz at en.wikipedia

File:Example.of.complex.text.rendering.svg *Source*: http://bibliocm.bibliolabs.com/mwAnon/index.php?title=File:Example.of.complex.text.rendering.svg *License*: Public Domain *Contributors*: Bayo, Imz, Waldir, Wereon, 1 anonymous edits

File:Sapta Chakra, 1899.jpg *Source*: http://bibliocm.bibliolabs.com/mwAnon/index.php?title=File:Sapta_Chakra,_1899.jpg *License*: Public Domain *Contributors*: Abhishekjoshi, Davin7, Quibik, Redtigerxyz, Roland zh, TheMandarin

File:Muladhara.svg *Source*: http://bibliocm.bibliolabs.com/mwAnon/index.php?title=File:Muladhara.svg *License*: Creative Commons Attribution-Sharealike 3.0 *Contributors*: User:Mirzolot2

File:Swadhisthana.svg *Source*: http://bibliocm.bibliolabs.com/mwAnon/index.php?title=File:Swadhisthana.svg *License*: Creative Commons Attribution-Sharealike 3.0 *Contributors*: User:Mirzolot2

File:Manipura2.svg *Source*: http://bibliocm.bibliolabs.com/mwAnon/index.php?title=File:Manipura2.svg *License*: Creative Commons Attribution-Sharealike 3.0 *Contributors*: User:Mirzolot2

File:Anahata green.svg *Source*: http://bibliocm.bibliolabs.com/mwAnon/index.php?title=File:Anahata_green.svg *License*: Creative Commons Attribution-Sharealike 3.0 *Contributors*: User:Mirzolot2

File:Vishuddhi blue.svg *Source*: http://bibliocm.bibliolabs.com/mwAnon/index.php?title=File:Vishuddhi_blue.svg *License*: Creative Commons Attribution-Sharealike 3.0 *Contributors*: User:Mirzolot2

Image Sources, Licenses and Contributors

File:Ajna.svg *Source*: http://bibliocm.bibliolabs.com/mwAnon/index.php?title=File:Ajna.svg *License*: Creative Commons Attribution-Sharealike 3.0 *Contributors*: User:Mirzolot2

File:Sahasrara.svg *Source*: http://bibliocm.bibliolabs.com/mwAnon/index.php?title=File:Sahasrara.svg *License*: Creative Commons Attribution-Sharealike 3.0 *Contributors*: User:Mirzolot2

File:Crown Brow Throat Chakras, Rajasthan 18th Century.jpg *Source*: http://bibliocm.bibliolabs.com/mwAnon/index.php?title=File:Crown_Brow_Throat_Chakras,_Rajasthan_18th_Century.jpg *License*: Public Domain *Contributors*: Deadstar, Till.niermann, William Vroman

Image:ChakraDiag.jpg *Source*: http://bibliocm.bibliolabs.com/mwAnon/index.php?title=File:ChakraDiag.jpg *License*: Creative Commons Attribution 2.0 *Contributors*: Kim

Image:Yoga all chakras and chakraserpent.png *Source*: http://bibliocm.bibliolabs.com/mwAnon/index.php?title=File:Yoga_all_chakras_and_chakraserpent.png *License*: Creative Commons Attribution-Sharealike 3.0 *Contributors*: User:Mirzolot2

Image:Chakra07.gif *Source*: http://bibliocm.bibliolabs.com/mwAnon/index.php?title=File:Chakra07.gif *License*: unknown *Contributors*: GeorgHH, SockMonkey, 1 anonymous edits

Image:Chakra06.gif *Source*: http://bibliocm.bibliolabs.com/mwAnon/index.php?title=File:Chakra06.gif *License*: unknown *Contributors*: GeorgHH, SockMonkey

Image:Chakra05.gif *Source*: http://bibliocm.bibliolabs.com/mwAnon/index.php?title=File:Chakra05.gif *License*: unknown *Contributors*: GeorgHH, SockMonkey

Image:Chakra04.gif *Source*: http://bibliocm.bibliolabs.com/mwAnon/index.php?title=File:Chakra04.gif *License*: unknown *Contributors*: GeorgHH, Incnis Mrsi, Patrick, SockMonkey

Image:Chakra03.gif *Source*: http://bibliocm.bibliolabs.com/mwAnon/index.php?title=File:Chakra03.gif *License*: unknown *Contributors*: GeorgHH, SockMonkey

Image:Chakra02.gif *Source*: http://bibliocm.bibliolabs.com/mwAnon/index.php?title=File:Chakra02.gif *License*: unknown *Contributors*: Dodo, GeorgHH, SockMonkey

Image:Chakra01.gif *Source*: http://bibliocm.bibliolabs.com/mwAnon/index.php?title=File:Chakra01.gif *License*: unknown *Contributors*: GeorgHH, SockMonkey, 1 anonymous edits

The cover image herein is used under a Creative Commons License and may be reused or reproduced under that same license.

http://farm4.static.flickr.com/3086/2301302732_6e029d75fd_o.jpg

CPSIA information can be obtained at www.ICGtesting.com
Printed in the USA
LVOW051217150212